Islam and Judeo-Christianity

Islam and Judeo-Christianity

A Critique of Their Commonality

Jacques Ellul

Translated by D. Bruce MacKay
Foreword by David W. Gill
Preface by Dominique Ellul

CASCADE *Books* · Eugene, Oregon

ISLAM AND JUDEO-CHRISTIANITY
A Critique of Their Commonality

Cascade Books
An Imprint of Wipf and Stock Publishers
199 W. 8th Ave., Suite 3
Eugene, OR 97401

www.wipfandstock.com

ISBN 13: 978–1-4982–0410-1

Cataloguing-in-Publication Data

Ellul, Jacques.

   Islam and Judeo-Christianity: a critique of their commonality / Jacques Ellul, translated by D. Bruce MacKay.

   xx + 104 p. ; 23 cm. Includes bibliographical references.

   ISBN 13: 978–1-4982–0410-1

   1. Islam—Relations—Christianity. 2. Christianity and other religions—Islam. 3. Theology, Doctrinal. I. Title.

BP172 .E525 2015

Manufactured in the U.S.A.   08/12/2015

Previously published in French as *Islam et judéo-christianisme*. Paris: PUF, 2004. Republished PUF, Quadrige, 2006.

All Scripture quotations are directly translated from Ellul's version.

Permissions have been granted for reprinted chapters to this book by:
Eerdmans for the use of chapter 5 of *The Subversion of Christianity*
Bat Yeʾor for the foreword to *The Dhimmi: Jews and Christians under Islam*
Bat Yeʾor for the foreword to *The Decline of Eastern Christianity under Islam*.

Contents

Foreword

During the 1980s Jacques Ellul often spoke of a book he was preparing on Islam but said he found publishers reluctant to publish the sort of critical perspective he felt essential. Events also moved rapidly and his manuscript needed substantial updating after these publishers' delays. Now twenty years after the death of Ellul, the subject is more urgent than ever. If not a "clash of civilizations," we certainly have a clash of religions and political-religious ideologies. Conflicts posed in religious terms and rhetoric are heating up, not cooling down.

One thing you will not find in this collection of essays is any counsel or guidance on what to do about religious differences, specifically those differences between Islam and Christianity. We certainly cannot change the often tragic history of Islamic-Christian relations. And at some level we cannot change an irreducible conflict of ideas, beliefs, and foundational commitments. But what we can do is tell the truth, listen, repent, and find common ground. Nothing is gained by cowardice and avoidance. All is lost by arrogance and accusation. As St. Paul writes, we must "speak the truth in love." As St. John writes, "If we say we have no sin we deceive ourselves and the truth is not in us."

What we have in this little book are six essays on Islam by Jacques Ellul and commentary on what it all means. The first three essays by Ellul form a heretofore unpublished manuscript he called "The Three Pillars of Conformism." These essays address three common assertions about Islam and its relations with Christianity and Judaism. In the first one, Ellul disputes the value of the assertion that "we are all the children of Abraham." The three "Abrahamic religions" are often claimed to share an affinity. Ellul insists that Isaac alone of Abraham's children received the divine and paternal blessing—not Ishmael or the other children. Moreover, according to Jesus, it is not blood lineage but living faith that renders one a true child of Abraham.

Second, Ellul disagrees that avowing "monotheism" brings Christianity, Judaism, and Islam into a close and positive relationship. To begin with, Muslims and Jews often dispute that trinitarian Christians are monotheists. More importantly, it is not the fact of having one god that unites people (other religions and even secular "religions" sometimes have one sacred center, one object of worship and center of meaning)? No, it is the identity of that God that decides everything. Ellul argues that the Muslim Allah is dissimilar to the God known in Jesus Christ and the Bible.

Third, Ellul rejects the idea that Islam, Judaism, and Christianity are united in being "religions of the book." It is partly about the nature of the holy writing and how it is viewed, which establishes big differences; it is supremely about the content of the books—including the ways the Koran contradicts the teaching of the Bible.

The fourth essay on Islam from Jacques Ellul, "The Influence of Islam," was published in 1984 as a chapter in *La Subversion du christianisme*.[1] Islam is but one of several factors and forces Ellul blames for undermining and distorting the faith of Jesus Christ over the centuries. But he does argue that the encounter of Christianity with Islam after the seventh century influenced Christianity toward holy war and the crusades, a reduction in the status of women, an acceptance of coercion as a means toward conversion, the practice of colonialism, the reduction of living faith to legalism, and the mingling of religious and political law. He does not deny that Islamic civilization brought benefits to Christendom or that Christendom's faults and failures were of multiple origins, especially of its own making. But he wants to correct a revisionist

1. Ellul, *The Subversion of Christianity*.

history that portrays Islamic civilization as almost uniquely a benevolent force.

The fifth and sixth essays by Ellul are two extended prefaces or introductions to scholarly studies by historian Bat Ye'or: *The Dhimmi: Jews and Christians under Islam* and *The Decline of Eastern Christianity under Islam: From Jihad to Dhimmitude*. Ellul defends Bat Ye'or's research, which carefully examined a long history and found that Jews and Christians had a varied experience under Islam, some good, some bad situations. It is not correct to say that they were always protected and flourishing under Islam (today's politically correct viewpoint), nor were they always persecuted.

In sum, Ellul's six essays display his typical erudition—as well as independence—in ranging over both the theory (the theology and beliefs), and the historical practices and experiences of Islam and Christianity (and to a lesser extent Judaism). The preface to the French edition and an additional commentary add to the value of this volume. Jacques Ellul's daughter Dominique provides her take on how her father's views on Islam relate to the rest of his life and work, especially that concerning Israel and Judaism. His work protecting Jews with the French Resistance during the German occupation and his standing against the chattering intellectual classes in France as *Un Chretien pour Israël*[2], as one of his book titles puts it—and his rethinking of Israel's place in Christian theology in *Ce Dieu injuste . . . ? Théologie chrétienne pour le peuple d'Israël*[3]—are a critical part of the background. Recently some more of Ellul's essays on Israel have been collected and published under the title *Israël: Chance de civilization.*[4] Dominique does not provide a dry scholarly voice but that of a respectful, knowing daughter. We owe her a great debt for this and for her work with her older brother Jean to bring these essays to publication.

The added commentary was written as the foreword for the French edition of this book by distinguished historian and professor Alain Besançon. Besançon's lengthy essay is less a close

2. [*A Christian for Israel*]
3. [*An Unjust God?*]
4. [*Israel: Civilization's Lucky Break*]

commentary on Ellul's ideas than Besançon's own very complementary perspective on Islam. Ellul is certainly a minority voice on this topic but Besançon shows that he is not alone.

Ellul's writings on Islam display his usual passion and intensity. He is taking an unpopular position in a French intellectual milieu that, partly out of guilt over a colonial past and the presence of large numbers of impoverished Muslim immigrants, has tended to go to extremes and almost glorify Islam in an uncritical way. This is a context in which straight talk and candid opinions can be difficult. Even a strong supporter of Ellul such as Stéphane Lavignotte in *Jacques Ellul: L'espérance d'abord*,[5] takes him to task for overkill on the Muslim question. I have to admit that of all Ellul's writings this one makes me cringe the most. And yet I fully believe we must welcome Ellul's views on Islam in this new book no matter how uncomfortable they are. The stakes are too important. Let Ellul put the cards on the table.

What new readers of Ellul need to be aware of is that he was by nature and choice very dialectical in thought and expression. What this means is that truth is best discovered by highlighting the extremes, by accentuating contrasts—not by prematurely smoothing out contradictions, paradoxes, and awkward conflicts. Ellul enjoyed freely expressing in extreme form either pole in a given controversy—especially if he felt that one perspective was being neglected. If anyone uncritically loves technology or urbanization, just let me introduce you to Mr. Ellul! So Ellul's criticism of Islam is harsh. But remember that Ellul wrote ten times as much in harsh criticism of the subversion of Christianity, of its mediocrity, conformism, and guilt. And his critiques of the "religions" of Technique and Money are even stronger.

In any case, Ellul had no use for violence or nationalism (common reactions to fears of Islam or Christianity in today's world). In practice, he was a kind, humble, welcoming, listening man. One of his best friends was Rabbi Andre Chouraqui, the sometime chief rabbi of both Jerusalem and France, who translated the Hebrew Bible, New Testament, and Koran—and who explored Islamic

5. [*Jacques Ellul: Hope First*]

understandings of the ten commandments alongside those of Jews and Christians.[6] Robust debate and total frankness are the preconditions for human interaction and community, not their enemy.

In my view Yale Professor Miroslav Volf's *Allah: A Christian Response* is an essential companion to Jacques Ellul's *Islam et judeo-christianisme.* Ellul provides a challenge to rethink Islam (and Judaism and Christianity), to cast off political correctness and comforting myths we may hold, to face the truth with courage, to speak with candor, and then to move forward toward a genuine peace and understanding. Volf demonstrates how such an encounter might proceed in peace. In the end, we must not just identify our differences; we must learn to live with them in peace.

David W. Gill[7]
Boston, December 2014

---

6. Chouraqui, *Les dix commandements aujourd'hui.*

7. David Gill is founding President of the International Jacques Ellul Society (www.ellul.org) and currently Mockler-Phillips Professor of Workplace Theology and Ethics at Gordon-Conwell Theological Seminary.

Preface

Jacques Ellul, lawyer, historian, sociologist, and Protestant theologian, who died in 1994 aged eighty-two, has left us a considerable body of work (fifty-three books and a thousand articles translated into some ten languages). He was not well recognized in the intellectual circles of Paris as a sociologist or in the world of the Reformed Church as a theologian. However, in the United States, he was seen to be at the forefront of French intellectuals in view of his work on technology,[1] his biblical textual studies, and his *Ethique de la Liberté*[2] in three volumes. When he taught at the University of Bordeaux, his students appreciated his courses on the history of institutions, Marxism, and propaganda, but also his humanity. Those who met him remember his commitment and his struggle as a man of faith, a faith with multiple implications for social and political life.

His thought is structured around two main themes: on the one hand, critical analysis of problems generated by the exponential increase in the technological phenomenon, and on the other hand a Christian ethics of freedom and hope appropriate for this technological society. His original work has inspired intellectuals and politicians of opposing views. Indeed, some internationalists still claim to be influenced by him, as do those Christians and Jews who support Israel. Contrary to what some might think, these two

1. *La technique* strictly means technique or the technical order. This same meaning applies in the use of the word "technological" in the following paragraph also.

2. Ellul, *The Ethics of Freedom*.

themes have a somewhat disturbing unity. They meet, explain, and complement each other. It is therefore inappropriate to dissociate them—precisely because this bringing together of the two themes, based entirely on the prophetic testimony of Ellul, is unique. Patrick Troude-Chastenet, in a book published six months after Ellul's death, wrote,[3] "Whether or not we discuss or even refute Ellul's analyses, we can no longer fail to be aware of them." Jean-Claude Guillebaud also mentions "Jacques Ellul the Great Disturber" in his writings.

This publication, *Islam and Judeo-Christianity*, comprises a central text, which Ellul entitled, "*Les trois piliers du conformism.*"[4] This hardly decipherable, fifty-page manuscript, which has not been published previously, is part of a continuity of writings by Ellul on this theme and was probably written towards the end of 1991, since at intervals between the years of 1980 and 1991, he produced several writings dealing with the three "religions of the Book."

The second text, which is added to this book as an appendix, is a foreword to a well-researched book *The Dhimmi: Jews and Christians under Islam,*[5] on the problem of dhimmitude—the conditions of Jews and Christians living in a Muslim society. It was written by a specialist on the subject, Bat Ye'or, and published in 1985 in the United States. This foreword, written in 1983, has never before been published in French. It is all the more important because it relates to the chapter devoted to Islam in Ellul's book *Subversion du Christianisme,*[6] written in the same period. In the context of dhimmitude, Islam is presented as a legal and political religion, with a nonprogressive character and a universal application, that has assigned to the subjugated peoples an inferior status comparable to that of the serf in the Middle Ages. In chapter 5 of *Subversion du Christianisme,* Islam is portrayed as a nonprogressive, totalitarian religion, founded on the concept of divine right,

---

3. Chastenet, *Sur Jacques Ellul.*

4. *The Three Pillars of Conformism.* This is Ellul's title to the manuscript that forms the basis for the current work—*Translator.*

5. Ye'or, *The Dhimmi* (foreword by Ellul).

6. Ellul, *The Subversion of Christianity.*

and credited with having introduced into Christianity the idea of holy war, i.e., the idea that war may be good. Thus, Jacques Ellul distinguishes a primary theological disagreement between Islam and Christianity, the former being based on law, expression of the divine will, and essentially warlike political power; the latter on grace which is theologically the opposite of law—law being considered a necessary evil. In this respect, it is important to emphasize that there is a difference between law and ethics.

Both these accounts, supported with historical facts, reinforce the idea that Islam represents "a permanent military threat to the West"[7] and that the Islamic world has not evolved in the way it regards the non-Muslim, "which is a reminder of the fate in store for those who may one day be submerged within it."[8]

In 1984, in the context of the war in Lebanon and the PLO Charter stipulating a programmed elimination of Israel by the Arab states, Jacques Ellul wrote *Un chrétien pour Israël*.[9] This book is a history lecture doubling as a lecture on Christian faith. One chapter is dedicated to propaganda, and in it, all the ingredients of the worsening conflict are already included. Here we rediscover the spirit and the rigor of Ellul, the historian of institutions and writer of two works on propaganda.[10] The book ends with a poignant call to pray for the Chosen People's survival: "A Christian for Israel, what is he? He is nothing, a reed that quivers in the wind, a leaf rustling; he writes one book among a hundred thousand books, and bitterly he knows that this book may be used for all sorts of propaganda or misunderstood by all those with different opinions. It is an attempt that will not push the boundaries in the course of political time. But nevertheless this must be done, because a Christian for Israel is first and foremost a man who lives in the Hope of the Lord, and who prays."

7. Ibid., 95.

8. Foreword (unpublished in French), to the US version of Bat Ye'or, *The Dhimmi*, 33. (See the appendix to this book.)

9. [*A Christian for Israel*]

10. Ellul, *Propaganda*; and Ellul, *Histoire de la propagande* [*History of Propaganda*].

In 1991, a sequel to *Un chrétien pour Israël* was published as *Ce Dieu Injuste? Théologie chrétienne pour le peuple d'Israël.*[11] In this essential book, the three religions have a specific place. The Hebrew people are the witnesses to the action of a liberating God, freed as they have been from slavery, and they have been elected to communicate his love to humankind through the expression of the Law revealed to Moses. Christians are the "grafted in" witnesses, messengers of the faithfulness and love of God; they are people designated to testify concretely to the divine love mediated by the "non-power" of Jesus Christ, and to show humankind evidence of universal salvation, forgiveness, and victory over the powers of death by the resurrection of the Savior Jesus Christ.

Inspired by Rosenzweig, Jacques Ellul defines Islam as "a new testament without the old." Covered with a biblical veneer, Islam seems deeply permeated with idolatrous and pagan practices, and anti-Semitism. It is important to recognize that when Christians worship idols, are violent or anti-Semitic, they are at odds with their founding text. This is not the case in Islam. In *Ce Dieu Injuste?* Jacques Ellul recalls that the ignominy of anti-Semitism is not only hatred of the Chosen People of God, but also "hatred of the project of God."[12] According to Ellul, the Jewish people are a direct link with universal redemption, and the enigma of their existence and suffering is a direct link with the end of history.[13]

The book *Ce Dieu Injuste?*, along with this current volume, *Islam et judéo-christianisme*, deliver the full vision of Jacques Ellul's theological thinking on the three monotheistic religions. The first book in particular focuses on the relationship of Judaism with Christianity and the second on the relationship of Judeo-Christianity with Islam.

In the same period and within the time frame of the first Gulf War, Jacques Ellul wrote *Les trois piliers du conformisme* as well as the foreword to Bat Ye'or's second book on *jihad* and dhimmitude.[14]

11. Ellul, *An Unjust God?*
12. Ibid., 81.
13. Ibid., 82.
14. Bat Ye'or, *The Decline of Eastern Christianity.*

Les trois piliers du conformisme poses the global problem of the sudden enthusiasm of intellectuals for Islam. The introduction sets out three chapters of a theological nature with the respective titles: "Nous sommes tous les fils d'Abraham," "Le monothéisme," and "Des religions du livre."[15] Today, these three concepts, which misrepresent deep theological meaning to serve ideological ends, constitute the three pillars of this new conformism. In this regard, we note in these titles that ironic twist of which Jacques Ellul was particularly fond, and we can distinguish a reference to the "five pillars of Islam," which are the five practices of the Muslim religion. The title *The Three Pillars of Conformism* is also an allusion to the title of T. E. Lawrence's book, *The Seven Pillars of Wisdom*, which was a great "hit" at the time in Parisian circles. Col. T. E. Lawrence sided with the Bedouin to free the Arabs from the Turks, and his book relates these struggles in detail. In the final analysis, *The Seven Pillars of Wisdom* has no relationship with the "seven pillars" cited in the book of Proverbs 9:1, but rather sets this epic story against a backdrop of the Arab aspiration for independence. Of course, it did not fail to fascinate Western intellectuals at the time, molded as they were by good feelings towards Islam and guilt feelings for having been colonizers.

The third and final text mentioned, the foreword to Bat Ye'or's book *Chrétientés d'Orient entre jihâd et dhimmitude*,[16] is in the other field of discourse familiar to Jacques Ellul—the sociological field. It summarizes all the arguments Ellul had already raised on this issue. It focuses on jihad as the main theme of the book. Jihad is fundamentally distinct from traditional war in that institutionally it aims not to restore peace, but to reproduce itself. On the other hand, the argument for jihad as a "spiritual war" (with oneself), the author does not find convincing, in that it is made by a minority group which is pacifist and by definition vulnerable. At the end of the article, Ellul lays out some introductory groundwork to this huge problem that is obviously of major political and

15. "We Are All Sons of Abraham," "Monotheism," and "The Religions of the Book."

16. Bat Ye'or, *The Decline of Eastern Christianity*.

social interest in the current climate. Therefore, I would like to quote the final lines of Jacques Ellul on this subject: "Certainly, many Muslim Governments attempt to combat the Islamist trend, but to succeed would require a total recasting of the way people think, a desacralizing of *jihad*, a self-critical awareness of Islamic imperialism, an acceptance of the secular nature of political power, and the rejection of certain Koranic dogmas. Of course, after all the changes that we have seen taking place in the Soviet Union, this is not unthinkable. But what a global change that would imply: the change of a whole historical trend and the reform of an immensely structured religion!" Jacques Ellul the historian completes this foreword by reminding us "history does not repeat itself."

At the end of this introduction, let us note that the text *Les trois piliers du conformisme* was published ten years after the death of Jacques Ellul on the initiative of his son Jean, who sent the manuscript to David G. Littman, historian and friend of Jacques Ellul, to prepare a final version. We particularly thank David G. Littman for all his work deciphering and preparing, and his kind contribution, making the process of publication a smooth one. We would like to express our keen gratitude to Alain Besançon for his remarkable foreword[17] that confers on the work of Jacques Ellul an historical value of major importance. The final remarks in his foreword add to the subject a warm, friendly tone that cannot leave unmoved those who knew Jacques Ellul.

By way of a postscript, I add that Jacques Ellul received the title of "Righteous among the Nations" as a posthumous tribute from the Yad Vashem Foundation in Jerusalem in July 2002 for assisting, at his own risk and peril, Jewish refugee families during the Nazi occupation.

Dominique Ellul

17. Alain Besançon's foreword forms the Appendix to this English edition—*Translator*.

Acknowledgments

I discovered Ellul's work in about 1975 and over a number of years developed a great respect for him. Eager to read other works of Ellul, I embarked on a translation of Ellul's *Islam and Judeo-Christianity* for my own purposes and for its topicality. However, the opportunity for publication came after meeting Ted Lewis (of Wipf and Stock Publishers) at the 2012 Ellul conference in Chicago.

I would like to thank several people who assisted me with the English translation. A friend in Oxford, England with a lifetime of French translation and work at the Sorbonne in France offered to review the translation and then assisted me in completing the translation. However, she wished to remain anonymous. Russell Armitage, a New Zealand "wordsmith," provided valuable feedback and review on the flow of the English translation at the early stages of the translation and then again at the final stages.

Anne-Marie Andreasson-Hogg carried out preliminary review for the quality of the translation, David Gill wrote the foreword, and Ted Lewis gave me valuable advice and assisted me with the publication process.

Bruce MacKay
New Zealand

Part I

Three Pillars of Conformism

Introduction

For nearly a decade, French intellectuals, generally speaking, have been seized with an excessive affection for Islam. We constantly read the praises of Islam at all levels: an absolutely ultimate religion, culturally rich, with profound humanism and spiritual devotion. Of course, all this is contrasted with the vulgar materialism of our barbaric civilization, our thirst for money, our passion for work, and our dehumanizing technology. On several occasions I have read that the victory of Poitiers in 732 AD, where the "Saracens" were crushed, was a disaster for civilization, that the Arabs were a thousand times more civilized than the barbaric French at the time of Charles Martel, and that if the Arabs had defeated the Barbarians we would have benefited from a far superior civilization, culture, and social organization. The distinction of the Kingdom of Granada is emphasized, for art as well as for literature, and unfortunately, it was once again the northern Barbarians who managed to defeat a beautiful creation. I have also read that we should apply ourselves to the school of Muslim wisdom and spirituality; there we would find the answer to, and a recompense for, the intolerable meaninglessness of the West.

Some have bravely undertaken to counter the "myths" invented by Westerners about the massacres that are supposed to have been perpetrated by Arabs and Turks in their conquests. Others have tried to prove that, all along, it was the Europeans who tried to provoke divisions between the Arab countries. They have gone so far that I have read that it was the Europeans who crisscrossed the Mediterranean plundering the coasts and not the Barbary pirates; and furthermore, using a remarkable argument, that Barbarossa, one of the great leaders of the "pirates," was a European! A friend of mine—a remarkable intellectual—told me that the Koran was "the grandest and most perfect of the world's poems." I could continue this enumeration of testimonies to the fervor and admiration of many French intellectuals for Islam. Not to be behind the game, I also plunged into the Koran, into a small digest of Hadiths, into books about Islam, until finally, I found that all that had been promised me amounted to nothing. However, I am well aware that it is quite pointless to discuss intellectual passions of this order, and that it would be a massive task to analyze the three-way correlation "Koran–Muslim societies–conquests." The study of the facts of conquest, and of the situation of the defeated, exceeded my competence,[1] as did moreover a serious study of the Koran, which must be read in Arabic if you are not to produce glaring misinterpretations.[2] For me, there still remained the insoluble question: How could generations of scholarly Arabists have so radically misinterpreted Islam, as to present it as a terror and a threat? How was such unanimity of opinion reached about the Islamic conquests (which we are now told is based on inaccurate facts); how could generations of people living on the edge of the Mediterranean have lived in terror of the Barbary pirates, etc., etc.? How public opinion reached this long-standing conclusion, which today is considered completely false, remains a mystery that I have never seen explained or even referred to.

Today, we have successfully "rectified" the situation and restored the "truth." The Koran is a book of prayers that is highly

1. This gap is now filled by the essential works of Bat Ye'or, of which the last, *L'Occident entre djihad et dhimmitude*, is radical. (Jacques Ellul here gives the original title of the manuscript of Bat Ye'or for which he wrote a foreword. The book was published in September 1991 as *Les Chrétientés d'Orient entre Jihad et Dhimmitude: VIIe–XXe siècle*. [*The Decline of Eastern Christianity under Islam. From Jihad to Dhimmitude: Seventh–Twentieth Century*]—Editors.) [See also the appendices—*Translator.*]

2. My friend Jean Bichon, who was a leading Arabist and who knew the Koran perfectly, has left some indisputable and critical articles.

mystical. (Everyone now knows this, because it has been explained to us that holy war, *jihad*, is not a war against enemies, but a spiritual battle that must be undertaken within oneself.) The Muslim "conquests" were entirely peaceful, and vague descriptions are generally preferred. (Thus, the *Encyclopedia Universalis*[3] says, "From the 7th to the 11th Centuries Islam spread . . ." but carefully avoids saying *how*. It "spread" by itself, magically, spiritually . . . .) As for the massacres and the oppression of Christian peoples, etc., all those are legends, spread in the West to justify our conquests, because the culprits in this story are we Europeans! We hear at length about the Crusades, that horrible intervention of Europeans in the peaceful Middle East, but no mention of the Arab conquests of the Byzantine Empire! Thus, we are witnessing a rewriting of the past, and of history that is entirely favorable towards Muslim peoples, a reinterpretation of the Koran, and a willing receptiveness to all the intellectual or spiritual trends in Islam.

We nevertheless have to wonder what is behind such a profound and dramatic change. For such a "conversion," one reason is insufficient, and we must look for an interplay of various factors.

A first clear fact is the presence of a very large number of North Africans, apparently five million[4] in France. We can no longer consider these peoples remote and foreign, and thus with no connection to us. We are obliged to have relationships with them. However, the most obvious fact, which we keep hearing, is that they are essential to the French economy. We are not far from the assertion that the whole economy is based on their work. If the North Africans were not there, everything would collapse, the French clearly being unable to work. Of course, it could never have been us doing a favor ("France, land of asylum, which takes in the unfortunate, the politically persecuted, and those from countries too wretched to maintain their populations"); it is these foreigners doing us a huge favor, and we must be grateful to them. Furthermore, they often perform work that the French no longer want to do, the most tiresome, abhorrent jobs. Therefore, they

3. The French equivalent of *Encyclopaedia Britannica*—*Translator*.
4. At the time of writing in 1991—*Translator*.

are "the poor" (even if they have enough money to send to their families remaining in the country of origin, as everybody knows very well). They are the poor of our opulent society (although it is noteworthy that we do not find any of these people among the "down-and-outs"). So the softhearted, especially Christians, are moved to assist them and are open to all their requests. Besides, they are foreigners ("You will treat the foreigner as one of your own," Christians remember), and therefore you should provide greater assistance to them than to others.

Yes, this may all be true, but how does it affect our changing understanding of Islam, our openness to it? Most often, these immigrants are only nominally Muslims. Just as 50 percent of the French are "Catholic"—they perform the rituals, recognize the celebrations and holidays, but that is all. In order to understand the reality, it is necessary to take account of the phenomenon that I have examined elsewhere, of "the endurance of religions." That is to say, someone who belongs in name, by tradition or by family, to a religion, is always likely to revert to being a religious devotee and sometimes a fanatic, if they undergo a "shock": persecution, an awakening emanating from a small mystical group, or injustice in a country practicing another religion, etc. Traditional rituals make humans open and receptive to a religious revival. And this is currently the case in France at least. On the one hand there is the fact of being immersed in a secular society—inconceivable for a person raised in an Islamic world—and on the other hand, we know that more or less everywhere there is an Islamic awakening. Moreover, dissemination of this information about Islam by the media takes on proportions that perhaps belie reality. (For example, in Algeria, the F. I. S.[5] is a tiny minority moderated by the authorities, but in Algerian circles in France, it is very influential.) These two factors help to reinvigorate Islam among North Africans in France.

As a result, we have here a set of factors that together impose the Muslim phenomenon on the media, intellectuals, and populations living in contact with North African groups. However, this development takes on a new importance. A Jewish or Protestant

5. Algerian Resistance—*Translator.*

6

group poses no problems; it is something ancient and established. These groups are not novel or surprising, so their beliefs do not attract our attention. Whereas, attention is drawn to Muslim beliefs, and our intellectuals can only try to discern, with different levels of understanding; so, they are drawn to what appeared insignificant thirty years ago (when only specialists were interested in Islam), but is now critical. And the impact is all the greater, because we have a guilty conscience towards Third World peoples from all points of view: a guilty conscience because we were conquerors ("colonizers") who justified ourselves by saying we were bringing civilization, whereas we were destroying vigorous cultures; and a guilty conscience, because as colonizers we exploited the colonized.

It is certainly an overstatement to say that Europe's economic boom is only due to exploitation of Third World riches, but it remains true that in some areas, raw materials from the Third World, acquired at a shamefully low price, have served Western "development." And so intellectuals, including quite a few Christians, have a guilty conscience, thereby feeling sympathy for everything African, North African, or from other Third World areas.

All the same, I shall add rather a malicious point: this bad conscience was nonetheless born the moment we were defeated by the colonized peoples. As long as we were strong, we retained the good conscience of a "civilizer." Interest in the North African peoples, for example, is aroused by their victory, their military power, just as the interest in the peoples of the Middle East coincides with oil power and the 1973–1974 oil crisis. And, for example, the war in Iraq was in fact a real success for the Arab world because it was necessary to mobilize all of American power to prevail against Iraq. Therefore, respect, very great respect, is due: we are no longer the strongest.

Thus, everything comes together, making us focus on the Arab phenomenon and arousing our interest: good will towards the North Africans—simple exploited laborers, Western guilty conscience for the past, and respect for new military strength. This interest concerns all things Arabic, including their religion, which at the same time reemerges in all its intransigence among the Arabs themselves, as we noted above. This then is the general phenomenon. The more specific fact is the trend towards adherence to this religion.

I will first take the case of the majority of the French secular and free thinkers: as long as secularism was a struggle and an ideal, it gave meaning to the lives of those who fought the (mainly Catholic) church. But, since secularism, the Republic, and agnosticism are well established, they are not very interesting! Yet, this is accompanied, in our inconsistent society, by several significant facts. A moral framework hardly exists anymore, i.e., morals in the broadest sense of a duty to be done, and not just of conformism. We no longer believe in any values; patriotism and socialism are well over and done with. We no longer believe in anything. We have no higher purpose, because making money or obsession with speed does not suffice to give meaning to life. However, so that the reader does not misunderstand, I attach no value to ideologies (I know how dangerous they can be, e.g., Nazism and Communism); I merely note that no society can remain without a set of common beliefs and without some ideology that provides cohesion. And suddenly, like a miracle, we have here a strong belief, with an entire corpus that gives meaning: a proclaimed truth, rites, a specific morality, absolute behaviors, intransigence, etc. How can we not be attracted by this excess of resources filling our void? Of course, fundamentalists are frightening; but there are now around us so many pious Muslims and pleasant interactions—therefore after all, why not amity? Intellectuals find a new opportunity for meaning and truth (while denying the religious character of that truth); and Muslim philosophers provide so many treasures; they have already so illuminated us without our knowing it—Al-Kindi, Al-Farabi, Avicenna, Averroes—furnishing all that is necessary to escape the monotonous Hegelian quarrel! In other words, on every level, the arrival in strength of the Muslim world in the West appears less as a danger than as an opportunity for reviving our culture.

Having completed this brief overview we have still to discuss Christians. They also know the attraction, caused by the physical proximity, the seriousness, the demands of this religion, and so many apparent resemblances. Symposiums between Muslims and Christians abound. Moreover, those I have attended are very restrained in their assertions. This is no longer an undiluted, tough Christianity, which affirms itself as such. During one of these conferences, I heard a dialogue on God between a renowned Catholic theologian and a Muslim one, without any reservation as to the God in question, and at the end of this discussion, the name of Jesus Christ had not even been mentioned. Christians, in addition to all the reasons I raised above, are still attracted to a religion that is uncompromising, unwavering, and rigorously logical in the extreme, while featuring illustrious mystics. These Christians feel the flabbiness of the common creed, the general disinterest in Christianity (while noting that in our society there is great need to believe, to find meaning).

In churches, congregations are declining. There is little effort at evangelizing; groups ancillary to the church are disappearing one by one. They have tried to attract younger members, but young people are interested in everything except church. They have wanted to modernize the liturgy, without thinking of the obvious, that is, that *only those who already attend services and masses* would know that this revised liturgy is more accessible or more vibrant. On the one hand, those outside the church do not know about it, and it does not attract them; it does not concern them anymore. While on the other hand, here is a wholly religious community (and Christians still place a value on the "religious"). I have also shown elsewhere the total opposition between religion and biblical revelation; I will not repeat it here.

Thus, Islam and Christianity are seen as on a par. Without doubt, these Christians are not ready to deny Jesus Christ—far be it from me to think such a thing! But apart from that, when there have already been so many other interpretations of the distinctiveness of Christianity, can we find common ground in order to understand or at least to hold a dialogue? Christians have begun to do this, and it must be said that it has been quite successful. Simply tone down certain characteristics, and do not directly face the judgment of Muslims on Christians and Jews, which has not changed. For a few years now, Christians have been undertaking this search for commonality, and it has been pretty easy. First unquestionably, these are monotheistic religions. Then, they are religions of "the Book"—a Holy Book in each case—what a godsend, what common ground! Finally, they recall that the Arabs are descended from Ishmael, and consequently we are all descendants of Abraham.

My decision to write this small work is due to the success of these three arguments, which state that Islam and Christianity are related. I will examine these three ideas, and I hope to show that this is all wind and that these words mean nothing.

1

We Are All the Sons of Abraham

To be sons of Abraham seems to be less important for Christian thought concerning Jews than for their thought concerning Muslims! This can be explained in that, in the case of the Jews it is a clear truth (with an important nuance that we shall discover), while with Muslims it is a somewhat subtle argument. Nevertheless, *Le Monde* (30 July 1991) published a fine article, entitled "Sons of Abraham in a Breton Reconciliation," which tells of a common pilgrimage by Christians and Muslims who celebrated *The Seven Sleepers of Ephesus* cult in a Breton hamlet. This pilgrimage is a remembrance of the martyrdom in the third century of seven young people, who, not wanting to deny their Christian faith, were taken to a cave in Turkey.[1] Muslims as well as Christians revere them, because their story is told in Sura 18 of the Koran. Hence the link: "we revere the same saints." Being a Protestant, I could point out that the "cult" (or worship) of saints is not Christian at all, in

---

1. This story, belonging to the Christian tradition, relates that in the third century, under the persecution of Emperor Decius [249–251 AD], seven young people took refuge in a nearby cave in Ephesus, where they slept for two centuries, woke up in the time of Emperor Theodosius II [401–450 AD], and died shortly thereafter. Later the Koran appropriated this story. Suras 18:8–26 are devoted to them. (Sourdel et Sourdel, *Dictionnaire historique de l'Islam* [*Historical Dictionary of Islam*]. Editor's note.) [Dates have been added for clarity—*Translator*.]

the biblical sense of the term; it appears very late in the primitive church and has no theological value: neither as regards grace and faith, nor as regards the Trinity, the resurrection, and above all intercession! Because it is with intercession that we diverge. Biblically, there is only one intercessor, Jesus Christ, who by his sacrifice alone redeemed all sins, who alone is seated at the right hand of God as Intercessor, and whose intercession alone is absolutely faithful, because it is directed from the Son to the Father. So, why would one want to add to this some other intermediaries?

There is no need for mediators to access the one and only mediator. Therefore, any cult of the saints is based on theological errors and is derived only from popular piety dating back to paganism, when people prayed to countless little local deities that were often transformed into saints.[2] In other words, the much-discussed close relationship identified between Christianity and Islam in this *Le Monde* article, relies on what is a popular but *non-Christian* feature of the cult of the biblical God and Jesus Christ.[3] This is just one example of what is becoming a cliché: "We are all Sons of Abraham." Let us then try to examine this formula a bit more closely. It is traditionally said that Arabs are descended from Ishmael. There is a story related in the Bible (biblical reference is legitimate because those who promote themselves as *Sons of Abraham* refer to the biblical tale), in which Abraham received God's promise that he would have a son. The important thing here is not the actual fact of this son; the drama does not play out around "having or not having progeny." Rather, Abraham has received a *special blessing* from God and the promise of countless progeny.

2. It was the habit in paganism to worship a little local deity, for instance a spring; it was the *genius loci* [the spirit of the place], and the missionaries appropriated the *genius loci* by assimilating it to a saint and transposing the popular discourse of the pagan *genius loci* to the Christian saint. Hence the countless: Saint Genis, Saint Genil, Saint Genesius, etc.

3. In conclusion, regarding this article, we learn a rather remarkable fact from the words of Father Michel Lelong at this meeting: "Whilst the integration of the Muslim community in France is a current issue, do not let us take three centuries to accept Muslims as we did Protestants." And there we have it—Muslims are made comparable to Protestants in "Christianity"!

The drama is twofold: "To whom will I pass on God's blessing?" and "Will God be faithful to his promise?"

In other words, is this God whom Abraham obeyed unceasingly a revealed and mighty God, or is he a deceptive God who does not keep his promises, and who is ultimately illusory? If God's firm promise to Abraham is not fulfilled, then everything that Abraham has founded his life upon collapses. Abraham finds waiting for fulfillment of the promise worthwhile. After the Word was heard, time passed, he grew older, but there was no son. Abraham was ninety years old and still God had not given him a son. Then, Abraham decided quite reasonably to do what was necessary. If there was no son, it was because his wife Sara had become sterile. What else would you expect from an old man and a sterile woman? What happened then may seem outrageous to us, but it was perfectly acceptable according to the customs of the time. He substituted a slave for the sterile wife (perfectly normal since the slave was fully identified with the master). Moreover, God did not disapprove of this union between Abram and Hagar; there was even a blessing and a promise for this son of Abram and Hagar. Everyone knows the story. Sara drove out Hagar, who fled with her son Ishmael and was saved in the desert by the angel. By this action, JHWH had already revealed himself as the God of all peoples, since Hagar was Egyptian. In addition, we might say that in response to Sara's hostility, Hagar's child was blessed by the angel, and also received a promise. However, the promise was extraordinary: he would have innumerable descendants (this is banal); but he would be like a wild ass,[4] he would be very violent, his hand would be against everyone, and everyone would be against him (but he would have innumerable descendants!). The assurance, therefore, registers in the real world, in history, but promises no peace, nor any covenant with God. What Abram believed would be fulfilled was not therefore just a pretence. It would take years until finally Sara had a son at a time chosen by God, and he appeared *entirely* as a child of the promise against all human possibilities. Isaac was a miracle child

4. Wild mule, but also war machine (Gen 16:12).

and his birth was as miraculous as that of Jesus. But thenceforth, on this child would rest God's blessing and promise.

What did this promise consist of? He would have (like Ishmael) many descendants. But this is not the most important thing. Rather in Genesis 18:17–19, there is a double promise. On the one hand, "in him all nations of the earth will be blessed"—can we imagine a more breathtaking reality? The child would now bear and pass on a blessing for all peoples of the world, present and future. The promise would be accomplished over a thousand years later in Isaac's ultimate descendant, Jesus Christ (and Zechariah,[5] in his canticle of Luke,[6] knew it well). On the other hand, the son carried and transmitted a perpetual covenant that God decided to establish with humans, a covenant that was also fulfilled in Jesus Christ. There is therefore a total opposition between Ishmael and Isaac. On the one hand, there is a temporal blessing maintaining human power, and on the other an eternal blessing, referring to the salvation of humanity, a covenant that finally will be fulfilled for all. Here is that promise of which Isaac was the bearer, and which must be passed from generation to generation. The opposition between the two sons results from Abraham's "error"! He received a promise of descendants, and he believed it. However, as I have said, the wait was long, and so Abram decided to fulfill this blessing through his own means. After all, it fulfilled God's promise! He was impatient, and would do what was necessary! Indeed, God did not condemn, he did not place any obstacle in the way of Abram's decision. No, Hagar had a son—that was very good— "God heard." But, if this human undertaking to fulfill a promise made by God succeeded on the human level (the child was born), it failed completely on the spiritual level. It was not Ishmael who received the blessing, the universal promise of a covenant between God and humankind.

---

5. Zechariah lived shortly before Christ. He was John the Baptist's father and his story in the New Testament recalls that of Abraham. He was a righteous man who observed the law blamelessly and although growing old, he still had no son. (Editor's note.)

6. Luke 1:5–23; 67–80.

Abraham in his impatience wanted to wrest from God what he had promised, instead of waiting for the time chosen by God, the moment, the hour (which is so often the same issue in the life of Jesus: "my time is not yet"). Moreover, God did not condemn him for having intended to do by himself what could come from God alone; he did not mock human effort, he placed no obstacles in the way. But—he maintained his freedom! The man thought he had succeeded, but this apparent success masked the fundamental failure, since the promise-blessing would not go to the one whom the man had chosen! Ishmael received a promise that was purely secular and concerned only his life (and thereby everyone's), but it is neither a universal promise nor a promise for eternity. In Isaac, *all peoples will be blessed*, and finally, after Israel's long history, all peoples will indeed be blessed in Christ, the offspring of Isaac, in whom the full scope of the covenant was fulfilled.

However, this is not the end of the Isaac-Ishmael relationship. Ishmael became a famous archer, and thus a fighter as had been prophesied. But earlier, Genesis adds a curious note to an event (Gen 21:8–9): Abraham held a feast the day Isaac was weaned, and at this point Ishmael began to laugh at Isaac, to ridicule him.[7] From the start, there was rivalry, and Ishmael, being the elder, believed he had greater rights than Isaac. In the end, we have here an assessment that establishes infinite distance between Isaac and Ishmael, who was the son of an Egyptian and who married an Egyptian. It should not be forgotten that Egypt, country of captivity, is also a terrible symbol: *mitsrahim*[8] means the land of Egypt, but also "the twofold anguish." It is exactly this that Ishmael bears in himself. Henceforth he is a constant threat to the descendants of Isaac. We can see that it is not enough to be a descendant of Abraham to have a positive and friendly relationship! Then there are other descendants of Abraham. After Sara's death, Abraham took as his wife, not Hagar, but Ketura, with whom he had six sons, who as

7. Ellul's translation "to laugh, to ridicule" differs from some modern translations, but it is consistent with Gal 4:29.—*Translator.*

8. The root of the word "mets" means that which oppresses, which tramples under foot, and "met-sar," singular of *misraïm*, means torment, anguish.

15

well as Ishmael, could compete with Isaac, but their descendants (except for the Midianites) were not in contention. So there are many other descendants of Abraham besides Jews and Arabs!

Finally, Isaac continues to be placed in a unique situation: it was he, when Abraham died, who received Abraham's *entire* inheritance. Nevertheless, I believe we must understand this legacy is not only material. Abraham's inheritance includes, along with his belongings, the promise and the covenant! This is indeed confirmed by God himself: "After the death of Abraham, God blessed Isaac, his son" (Gen 25: 11). Thus, being "descendants of Abraham" does not mean much, and we cannot draw any real conclusion about a relationship that would depend on a family connection or that might support a common *heritage* in the course of history. Now we have just seen that the *only* bearer of the heritage, covenant, and promise is ultimately Isaac! Therefore, at this level, the formula "we are also descendants of Abraham" means nothing.

However, we must also assess the scope of this expression. The Jews and the Arabs are not the only ones concerned. Christians are also (since this is about establishing the fundamental relationship between Christians and Muslims). Can we then simply say that all (nominal) Christians are sons of Abraham, that it is sufficient to be part of a church to be sons of Abraham, and that there is a kind of direct relationship between Christians and Abraham?

In reality, things are not so simple. In the Gospel or the Epistles, it is not a matter of "church members." It is firstly a matter of the one "who does good." This is found in the story of Zacchaeus,[9] a tax collector and therefore a Roman collaborator, earning his living by collecting taxes from the Jews. But, in contrast to what is often said, the tax collectors were not dishonest. They did not "steal" from the taxpayers. It was enough that they were part of a company of collectors[10] of such tax levies. They were either managers or simple collectors, which was the case of Levi (Matthew) in Luke 5:27. In the case of Zacchaeus, who was called "head of tax collectors," he was more likely to have been a manager of one of

9. Luke 19:1–10—*Translator.*
10. I.e., treasurers who organized the collection of taxes.

these companies. After the dialogue between Zacchaeus and Jesus, Jesus declared that Zacchaeus was actually a son of Abraham,
because Zacchaeus, who was "lost," still performed extraordinary
works (for example giving away 50 percent of his income, etc.!).
Then, regarding the works of Zacchaeus, Jesus declared that he
had come to search for and rescue those who were lost, and he
proclaimed him a son of Abraham. Which is to say not that Zacchaeus was saved by his works, but that his works bore witness to
him in such a way that Jesus declared that he was *a son of Abraham*
and was saved. In this declaration that bears witness to Zacchaeus's
salvation, it is not the works that have saved, but the *Son of Man*
who came to seek and save. This is already indicated in that he who
has "done good," i.e., fulfilled the will of God (by gift, mercy, concern for the poor, etc.), is *declared* a Son of Abraham (it is not, of
course, automatic). Now, it should not be forgotten that the major
"work" of Abraham is actually not of this order. It is faith in the
word of God (Abraham believed in God, in the word of God, and
that was credited to him as righteousness . . .)

By the same token, we can better grasp the reality of "Sons of
Abraham" when we read Jesus' decisive discussion with the Jews,
reported in John (John 8:39–40). Jesus announced to everyone,
"the truth will set you free . . . ." "But," replied those he was addressing, "we are sons of Abraham, and we have never been slaves
of anyone." "Of course," Jesus agreed, "you are the descendants of
Abraham, but you are looking to kill me, which means you do not
recognize the One who comes from the God of Abraham." The
Jews answered him, "Our father is Abraham." And Jesus replied,
"If you were children of Abraham you would do the works of
Abraham. Now you are looking to kill me, I who have told you the
truth that I have heard from God. This Abraham did not do!" In
other words, to be true descendants of Abraham is to perform the
same works that he did. We are back to the simple idea that a son
of Abraham is the one who does good. Jesus does not dispute the
physical relationship, the genealogy, but he disputes the spiritual
relationship marked by an attitude towards God (faith) and its
consequences (works).

Therefore, to declare "we are all sons of Abraham" means absolutely nothing. The question is who among Jews, Muslims, and Christians, performs the works of Abraham (which all come down to the consecration of an absolute faith, without limits, without weakening, in the God who is revealed). In other words, we cannot use arguments based on this sonship to proclaim the general kinship of Christians and Muslims! The "type" of relationship has nothing to do with an ancestral archetype and pedigree. Here we have entered a spiritual domain, and the works recommended by the Koran do not seem to me at all like those of Abraham!

Thus, we have seen the major difference between Jewish lineage and Arab lineage, and then between Christian lineage and Arab lineage. In other words, to proclaim that we are all sons of Abraham means no more than to declare that we are all children of Adam! It is an excessive, unfounded generalization to justify a kinship between Muslims and Christians.

However, I shall end on a wry note. In one of the discussions between Jesus and the Pharisees, reported by Matthew (Matt 3: 7–12), Jesus rejects the Pharisees. Firstly, he says, "Therefore produce fruits worthy of repentance, and do not presume to say to yourselves, 'we have Abraham as our father.'" We return to this fundamental truth that it is about the works of Abraham and not genealogical lineage. Then secondly, he adds ironically, "From these stones, God can raise up children to Abraham." There is perhaps a reference to the birth of Isaac here—it is just as easy for God to form children for Abraham from these stones as to decide to create Isaac!

Thus, the relationship with Abraham, in itself, is not significant. And this definitively refutes the famous proclamation "We are all sons of Abraham." It is unimportant, and creates no *real* link between us! This is all that we can infer from this close analysis of the expression!

2

Monotheism[1]

"We are all monotheists." Here is the ultimate argument, and the most stupid! We must try to dissect the issue. First, we have "Theos" or "God," but the word *God* is an empty word. We can make of it (and have made of it) anything at all. Everywhere, in all civilizations, there are one or more deities, and they never describe the same entity.

In the vaguest and most dubious way, it suggests that "something" higher than us exists, something powerful on which we depend. That this impression comes from fear, admiration, "natural" phenomena, the feeling that everything is ordered, or even that everything is foreseen in advance, and so on, is not important. I cannot understand the furious quarrels between those who believe in a transcendent God, a God who embodies natural forces, or a God who speaks through the mouth of a prophetess. This matters so little. Moreover, those who claim to be atheists or agnostics still refer vaguely (and sometimes explicitly) to destiny or fate, except when they replace the traditional God by their belief in science.

1. Islam violently opposes polytheistic religions such as Judaism and Christianity. That is why we speak *today*—because this expression, this grouping of "the three monotheistic religions" seems modern. [In the light of his comments later on in this section, it is evident Ellul does not mean to include Judaism here, whereas Islam classically understands trinitarian doctrine as polytheistic—*Translator.*]

The word *belief* is central. I am not saying that humans are religious animals, only that they are believers. This word "believe" applies to everything. We believe everything and everything is based on belief. What of scientific truths? In fact, I am obliged to *believe* them, because I am unable to prove by myself what has been demonstrated. In everyday relations, belief constantly plays a primary role. No communication is possible, nor is any conversation, if I do not believe what the other person is telling me. Even disagreement and debate are based on the belief that the other has something to say that is worth being discussed. If I do not believe, I shrug my shoulders and leave.

Here I will take two simple examples that seem to me to be characteristic of certain beliefs. Firstly, belief in the group: I cannot claim to live as Robinson Crusoe. I need a group to belong to, and one that allows me to have both human relations and ethical guidance in my family, trade union, corporation, political party, various associations, churches, and so on. At any rate, I must belong to a group and this group only plays its multiple roles of protection, consensus, and orientation for me if I believe in it! My attachment to the group is above all emotional! I think of a TV broadcast from 20 September 1991, where they were questioning activists on the crisis in the Communist Party. I was moved by the upheaval for these men. It was not an association that dissolved, but the truth that collapsed. Their past loyalty, their dedication, lost its meaning; the future no longer existed. None took the matter lightly; they had believed. And this recalled the dismay of some Christians when faced with the transformation of their church. People must believe in their group, and this gives a certain meaning and stability to life.

The other example is the set of what constituted "rustic beliefs" at the beginning of the twentieth century. These peasant beliefs, which concerned life and death, culture and relationships, all had an exactness, a relevance that we are gradually acknowledging today, having regarded them as superstitions. By quite another route, we have ended up adopting similar attitudes.

These small reminders of well-known facts are simply setting the necessary framework for speaking about this universal and persistent human phenomenon, i.e., religious belief. Nothing can destroy it, because whatever challenges it is immediately promoted to replace it, and becomes the subject of religious belief in turn. I have demonstrated this elsewhere for the sacred. The power that desacralizes a place, a counsel, a religion, is immediately sacralized in turn. It is exactly the same for whatever claims to destroy a belief. The destructive force immediately becomes the object of a new belief. This is obvious from the great secular offensive against "religion." In a very short time, secularity has become secularism and about a firm belief in values, an independent ethics, and a type of intellectual and even spiritual communion. Thus, the fact of belief seems inherent to human beings!

In this universe of beliefs, "religious" belief, which refers to an elusive beyond, is neither more nor less accentuated. There is no need to insist that people of various civilizations believed in multiple gods, as everyone knows this. Thus, the word "god" itself is meaningless and the phenomenon can be given multiple sociological, psychological, and psychoanalytic explanations. But religions have complicated the situation. In religions, there were people who went through inexplicable mystical experiences, coming undoubtedly from the "beyond," from the nonhuman realm. Others have reflected on this irresistible human phenomenon, of belief in a *transcendent*. And this thought, encountered by philosophers, has led to the discovery of a god who appears to be truly transcendent and therefore inaccessible. Starting from a belief, by a direct and innocent interpretation of the word *god*, we have managed to discover its limits. God has become a reality that cannot enter the human setting. In both Judaism and Christianity, and in a different way in Islam, we have access to a God who is inexpressible. We then go on to surround him in adjectives: the Merciful, the Almighty, the Unconditioned, the Absolute, etc., to mark the qualitative difference between what we continue to call God and what we have henceforth understood or discovered. But all this is completely inadequate. If God is truly God, he cannot be defined (i.e., located within certain limits), nor analyzed, nor proven.

The great debate on the evidence for the existence or non-existence of God is absolutely irrelevant, precisely because this God is beyond our grasp, our intelligence. And strictly speaking, all that I can intellectually prove exists is precisely not God but a representation. However, if God is God, by "nature" he cannot be proven in any sense, because this would mean that he is inferior to my intelligence, my means of investigation. If he is a subject for my reason, for my powers of investigation, he is precisely not the Transcendent, the Absolute, or the Eternal, of whom we cannot even conceive the reality! Because this is the expression of my intelligence, one could say I cannot even talk about it adequately! The Jews are quite right when they take the "true" name of God to be the unpronounceable JHWH. Quite simply, if they do not wish to misrepresent him, they will use oblique words: Adonai [the Lord] for example, or even more simply they will refer to him by saying: *Schem*, the "Name." However, when it is also necessary to speak about him, there is another nonspecific designation, the name *Elohim*,[2] which I will use; just as the word *God* is used. But we must confront the mismatch between what the word designates and the truth: the inadequacy of a designated reality and the *truth* that infinitely exceeds all that we can understand or feel, because with respect to God we have an uphill struggle for the truth. However, we must go one step further. The abstract word *God,* to designate what in German is called *Wirklichkeit,* is a very convenient word since it covers both reality and truth. It acquires its value only when we move from the question posed so far: "What is God?" to the much more radical question: "Who is God?" I am not satisfied only with knowing that there is this transcendent truth. It is not enough for me to name it; I must learn who it is.

And it is here that monotheism explodes! Because, if we can agree on the point that God is Unique, we part company as soon as we get any certainty on this "who." He is indeed not the same here as elsewhere. This is much more important than the notion of a transcendent absolute. Because now I go beyond the *objective*

---

2. See also Ellul's more detailed and relevant discussion of "Elohim" in *Reason for Being,* 214–31.—*Translator.*

and the *reflexive* to enter the existential: "Who is he?" This appears clearly in the debate between God and Moses. When God chooses Moses to go to his people and tell them they shall be freed from Pharaoh, Moses objects: "I will go to the children of Israel and will tell them, 'The God of your fathers sends me to you,' but if they ask me what his name is, what shall I tell them?" God says to Moses, "I am who I am." And he adds, "This is what you shall say to the children of Israel: he who is called 'I Am' sent me to you" (Exod 3: 11–15). Thus, the important thing is not so much to believe in a God, but to know his name.

Here we find that the bridge that we thought we could build between Islam and Christianity is undermined. Monotheism? Yes, but we have shown this means nothing! On the one hand, there is JHWH, God of Abraham and Jesus Christ, there is Jesus Christ who is God in and with the Father, and on the other hand, there is Allah.

We will try to clarify the correlation, the similarities, and the differences. But before that, it is obviously necessary to emphasize an important point of the debate. For Islam, Christianity is not monotheistic because of the Trinity.

It must be recognized that we have a terribly difficult issue, that it is impossible for any non-Christians (and often for thinking Christians) to understand that three equals one, and considering that for many Muslims, it is Mary who is the third character of the Trinity. However, therein lies the reason for confusion, in that "persons" are identified in the story of the Trinity. It is a diabolical idea to talk about three persons, because they are in fact "*ways of being God*"—God is himself his own counterpart. In God there are first and second elements (second does not mean less important). The "unity of God" does not mean closing off, solitude, and isolation. The unity of God is an open, free, and self-motivated unity, a dynamic unity. In Christ, for example, there is divine obedience. Therefore, God at the same time reigns and commands as sovereign, and obeys in humility. He is without any division or differentiation but is in perfect unity and equality, *because* he has three ways of being God. He is the God who asserts the unity and equality of his divinity in his first two ways of being without contradiction or separation. In addition, by virtue of the third way of being, he is God, in his entirety, in interdependence, and in the interplay of intradivine relations. Because any separation or contradiction is excluded, so is any tendency towards identifying the ways of being divine. God is God, in these inseparable and irreducible ways of being, which are neither metaphysical nor philosophical, but revealed by him in the book that tells the full story of "God-with-humans," as well as of "God-with-God."

He is therefore, in the revelation (and how else can we know him except by what he reveals of himself?), totally different from what we are used to calling "god," i.e., a neutral, pure, empty divinity. That, says Karl Barth, is the illusory masterpiece of an abstract "monotheism," which, at the height of the evolution of all primary religions, all mythologies, is a "'mockery of humanity." The true God, "the living God, is one whose divinity consists in a story and who is thus precisely *in his three ways of being*: one God, Almighty, Holy, and Merciful—the one who loves in his freedom and who is free in his love" (Karl Barth).[3] If we really wish to understand the Trinity, we need to recognize that it is not in opposition to unity. It is precisely this understanding of the Trinity that will now clarify and allow us to grasp, if not to analyze, the complex relationship between this God and humankind, a relationship that, never forget, expresses "love in freedom" and "freedom in love." His external action consists in his letting the world, and humanity whom he has created, participate in the story in which he is God. This means that the work of creation becomes a reflection or parable, where the creator and creature are counterparts, and the duality of the existence of human beings is an image of the internal life of God himself. Finally, at the end of divine action, what was implied at the start occurs: God himself, in his "way of being" characterized by obedience and humility, becomes human, among and for humans. The intradivine relationship between the one who commands and the one who obeys in humility becomes identical in the work of reconciliation, and in the relationship between God and

3. Barth, *Dogmatique*, vol. XVII, 59. [*Church Dogmatics*]

one of his creatures: a human. His action is the ultimate sequel to the internal story of God.

At this point in our discussion, we can now ask, "what relationship can there be between the biblical God and Allah?"[4] Firstly, there is an enormous split because of the incarnation. The biblical God leaves his heaven, his majesty, and his eternity, to give himself and become human. God is so great that he is never more God or more worthy of worship than when he renounces the "attributes" of his divinity (which is truly incomprehensible to those who cannot conceive of a god abandoning what we understood to be the attributes of God!). God thus has the possibility of presenting himself in another *real* guise, that of being himself in a second way different from the first: *in* us and *with* us, giving and giving himself. Furthermore, this God, at one and the same time, is he through whom everything exists. The acceptance of the coming of God, the gift God makes of himself, is not left to arbitrary, indifferent, or extraordinary human beings. Of course, man is respected by God, who did not make him into a robot; but when faith in this revelation of God-in-Christ is born, when man joyfully receives the gift of forgiveness and salvation, it is still by the action of God, by a third presence of God [the Spirit], who is the perfection of the love of the Father for the Son, and of the Son for the Father. For example, in the Psalms, when God is worshiped, proclaimed, and hymned by people, he and his work are revealed, and humanity's response is the work of God as much as a gift.

Now, all this is completely unacceptable in Islam. God is strictly unique, meaning that we have an "extrinsic" concept of his unity. He is unique as a work of art is unique. It is a matter of *numerical* not ontological unity. By ontological I mean, for example,

4. In all the amplifications on Islam and Christianity that follow, I was mainly inspired by Jean Bichon's handwritten notes, lecture notes, draft articles, and personal reflections. Also here I must pay tribute to this very learned Arabist and Islamic scholar, who could have had a reputation comparable to that of the greatest if he had published the kilos of notes he accumulated during his life spent in Muslim countries. But he never sought publication, from indifference or a perfectionist mind. Significantly, Bichon taught Arabic at the University of Algiers, after Algeria gained independence.

that the human being is one, and yet, according to the distinction commonly accepted by theologians, a person has a body, soul, and spirit, a trinity that our materialism has unsuccessfully tried to suppress. Just as a great scientist cannot find a soul under his scalpel, so he cannot find with his scalpel the complex and exaggerated motivations (with regard to biological functioning) that are integral to human life!

However, the Father-Son-Holy Spirit unity of the biblical God is "ontological." That is because the very Being of God, Creator, and Father (who does not with proud, indifferent power make a universe in his own "likeness") is so close to his likeness that he himself becomes Son, and he loves his creature so much that he gives himself to him through the Holy Spirit. Thus, the biblical God is no *less* one than the God of Islam, even if we do not have the same understanding of unity.

On the other hand, the God of Islam is so absolutely transcendent that he cannot have in any way a mutual relationship with man; there is no conceivable incarnation in this transcendence, because it is the ultimate mark of divinity, whereas the biblical God, the living God, is *love*. He is transcendent, yes, but with love that produces a link, a relationship between this transcendence and humanity! This is not conceivable in Islam and therefore incarnation is impossible: God "does not beget," just as he is obviously not begotten.

Neither can there be a personal relationship of God with man in Islam. God as "person" is sovereign and inaccessible. He arbitrates and judges the actions of humans without intervention; he does not love and thus does not himself cover the sins of man. God the judge is not at the same time God the "advocate" (Paraclete). Obviously all this great biblical Saga of God with humankind cannot connect in any way with an absolute Transcendent. Love is missing here. The feeling that God has for his creatures is missing. Therefore there is no redemption (and no redeemer!), no freedom recreated by God in the human heart, no "new heart," and therefore no ethics based on the personal relationship of a human with God. Thus, the name "God" conceals completely different meanings.

And the attributes recognized as being God's do not have the same meaning in Islam as in the Bible.

Let us consider two features: unity and transcendence. Firstly unity: "You believe God is one? You do well; the demons also believe and they tremble" (James 2:19). Biblically speaking, to believe that God is one God (and not several gods) is not false, but this idea remains extrinsic and alien to his person. God did not reveal himself to tell us *that*, but to communicate himself in his life and his mystery. This inner reality of God, this is whom we know when we contemplate the Son "who is in the bosom of the Father," and whom we receive with the Holy Spirit, "the life-giver."

Instead of this, Islam asserts that God is one in himself, to the point of refusing any diversity within him and relationship of him with himself. At this point, God's unity amounts to the inner void of the number "one." Consequently, what God (Allah) is for us has no more substance than what he is in himself (contrary to what we saw above for the biblical God). His action becomes completely arbitrary, and human morality, rather than being the fruit of liberation, culminates in fear and resignation. The radical divergence is obvious in the person and work of Jesus. In other words, instead of starting with a conception of God (to which we could also add details about Jesus, including his divine nature and his redemptive death), we have to establish just one foundation, Jesus Christ. The basis of Christian doctrine cannot be a doctrine of God, with a role or place for Jesus. Paul reminds us that the foundation *is* Jesus Christ, and that it is through him that we must begin and build.[5] On this occasion, Paul speaks of "building with straw." Without the basis of Jesus Christ, any theology is straw to burn, including the characteristics that we assign to God—unity, transcendence, eternity—that are also abstract ideas without content if they are not ordered in Jesus Christ. On the other hand, when we contemplate the Son, we receive the revelation of who God is.

Now consider the second point: transcendence. Allah's transcendence comes down to two elements: firstly, Allah is and remains separate from humanity by an infinite distance. Muslim

5. 1 Cor 3:12—*Translator.*

theology expressly rejects any idea of God moving towards humankind, or of his "descent." Secondly, from this infinite distance,
Allah makes decisions and acts towards humanity in a completely
unpredictable, arbitrary manner, and without any possible meeting between Allah and man. He reveals himself through a single
means—the prophets—but the common thread that connects the
prophets is an unchanging message: words and thoughts, fixed in
the same terms, because they are *reproducing* a pre-written, absolute, unique, and eternal book.[6]

Finally, we must always return to the fact that it is Jesus
Christ who prevents us from identifying the biblical attitude with
the Islamic attitude. It is not a matter of the same divine "unity,"
of the same "transcendence," or of the same action of God in history, because the presence or absence of the Lord Jesus Christ
completely changes the content of these very notions. Then the
Bible, in opposition to the Koran, speaks to us of a God of love, in
whom the Father and the Son love each other with an eternal love;
of a God who chose to exercise his transcendent omnipotence in
the extreme abasement and closeness of love; and of a God whose
revelation in history operates not by words, not by a pre-written
book, but by a personal encounter with a person.

To conclude, we say therefore that Muslim assertions about
God (his unity and transcendence), and about the historical character of his revelation to humankind are not a partial "truth," the
beginning, to be pursued and completed (the completion being
Jesus Christ). For it is *starting from Jesus Christ* (and not by adding
him as a "conclusion") that we learn about the unity of God, his
transcendence, and the meeting of God and the world. The truth
does not consist in words or in ideas (even very precise or scholarly ones), but in someone's living reality. When Jesus says: "I *am*

---

6. There have also been attempts to reconcile Islam and Judeo-Christianity
linguistically: Allah is also Eloah, which is the singular of Elohim. Thus we
have the same God: strictly speaking, Allah represents only one aspect of
which the plural Elohim reveals to us the diversity. I am not convinced: firstly,
because the singular is rarely used in the biblical text, and secondly because
we know enough of the kinship of Semitic languages not to be surprised at an
identity of terms that designate in a general manner . . . "God"!

the truth," he totally transforms what we can conceive of as truth. This is no longer a debate of ideas or philosophies, this is not science that leads to the discovery of truth; what scandalizes human intelligence is that the truth is not an abstraction, but *one* (and *only one*) person. For we need to understand that this does not mean that the words of Jesus are truths, or even that Jesus, by revealing how far both God's love and human love may go, expresses to us a primary truth, that of love. No. If his words are the truth, it is because *he* is the truth, and if his acts expressed the fullness of love, it is because the one who does them is the truth. And this is where we stumble. Yes, Jesus is a stumbling block. Either we believe that Jesus is the whole truth, and not an admirable example, nor a wonderful mystic; or we do not believe it. It all comes down to that. Consequently, it is pointless to admit this or that point. For example, to emphasize that the Koran acknowledges Jesus and even attributes miracles to him is irrelevant.

Incidentally, to note a detail that demonstrates the misunderstanding, none of the miracles reported by the Gospels is taken up in the Koran. However, the Koran attributes three miracles to Jesus. The first is that while "the child was still in the mother," he spoke—half mystically, half theologically. The second miracle, also reported in the apocryphal Gospels, is that of the infant Jesus producing small clay birds and making them come alive by blowing on them. The third, which also gives its title to the Sura describing it,[7] is that of the "table spread." People come to tell Jesus, "We will believe in you if you make a table of delicious food come down from the sky," so Jesus lifts his hands and the table comes down from the sky. This demonstrates much more than just a difference in stories. This is a fundamental difference in understanding. In fact, in the Gospels, *all* of Jesus' miracles are miracles of love, even those where he expresses "power." For example, in the "calming of the storm" he responds to the fear of his disciples. He performed this miracle to restore peace and confidence. But these miracles reported in the Koran are *exclusively* miracles of power. They are miracles that have no significance other than that of power. This

7. Koran, Sura 5.

reflects different ways of looking at what Jesus signifies in both texts. In addition, consideration must be given to a contradiction that confirms this: when the table is spread, they say to Jesus, "We will believe in you, if you perform this miracle." And Jesus does so. While in the Gospels, it is precisely whenever a miracle is proposed as a kind of test, that he refuses, and even more so, if they say they will believe in him "if . . .". It is just what Jesus does not want. He *is*, and it is, about a relationship of one person with another, not of miracle-working.

Finally, what expresses most of all the radically different way in which Jesus is understood by the Koran and the Gospels is the crucifixion. We know in the Gospels that Jesus pushes his love to its limit and after a tough spiritual fight accepts his death on the cross. However, in the Koran, it is unthinkable that he, whose power is his primary manifestation, should be crucified. Therefore, Jesus was not crucified (which avoids the question of the resurrection), but *it was another* person who was crucified in his place. We should dwell especially on this fact. How can we conceive of Jesus, who embodies the love of God, whose whole life was nothing but sacrifice, who becomes the prophetic "man of sorrows," in a nutshell this Jesus whose life *means nothing* if it does not constantly express God's love; how can we conceive of him as one who would have accepted another person being sentenced in his place, and crucified in his place? After all, he came in order to bear our condemnation and take on himself our suffering. After such a misinterpretation, you can say what you like about the presence of Jesus in the Koran and the respect that it shows for him, and *it means nothing*.

Therefore, to conclude this chapter we must say that, unlike what is often claimed, Islam is not a *Christian heresy* but a resolutely non-Christian religion, and that given this contradiction, there is no point in common. Thus Islam, when examined in the light of the Bible, is *no longer* a problem for Christian faith.

3

Religions of the Book

Here is the last big argument to bring together Islam and Christianity: They are "religions of the Book," that is to say that all of their truth, their basis, their *raison d'être* is in a book: the Bible or the Koran. How can we not reconcile two religions that have a similar basis, that have the same general orientation, that are religions based on *written documents*? We must try to examine this more closely. However, we can make a preliminary remark, which is that these two religions are not the only ones to be based on written documents. Elsewhere I have presented the theory of the founding book. *Mein Kampf* was certainly a book that founded a religion. And Mao's *Little Red Book* is unsurpassable. However, if we want to go beyond a very vague generality, we must try to compare them. Because, as we have just seen, in the end it does not clarify the issue to declare that they are religions of the Book. We must really ask, "What sort of book is it?" After all, any book can give rise to a passionate group that may become a cult. The key is knowing what gives rise to the credence that we place in such a book. I shall therefore try to make a comparison between the Bible and the Koran from several points of view, and not only on the content.

In fact, there is a primary radical contradiction with respect to their origins. On the one hand, we have a book written by a single man (except for perhaps a few insertions), and certainly not in one go, since parts were written at Medina and others in Mecca. On the other hand, we have a book compiled of layers from different times, written by dozens of authors, reshaped and sometimes synthesized (e.g., the different traditions collected after the Exodus to constitute the Pentateuch). For the Koran, the confirmation of its truth lies in the certainty that its content is inspired by God. The Bible has a complex story and its truth derives from the fact that a people, and then a church, received a message, examined it, and based on experience or debate in council, accepted or rejected it. It is a strange book where we see, preserved as the word of God, texts that condemn the very people who accepted it! Despite *apparent* contradictions (which are resolved when we understand how the texts should be read), a consistent and oriented way of thinking emerges from these writings that were written over about a millennium. There cannot be a greater difference with respect to the origins than this difference.

But in addition, and more fundamentally, the Koran claims it was "dictated" (letter by letter) by God to Mohammed, who was a simple recipient (faithful certainly, but on the whole simply designated as a recording device). Hence, of course, the Koran can be validly read only in Arabic, in the language chosen by God. In addition, the "mother" of the Koran is with Allah. Admittedly, there has also periodically been the temptation to believe that the Bible was dictated by God. There is a famous painting that depicts an angel dictating to an apostle what he is writing. But there is nothing in the Hebrew Bible or New Testament that allows us to infer that kind of inspiration. The only text that might have been of this type is the first Decalogue, but Moses broke the tablets. Apart from that, all the books of the Bible were written by accountable authors. They were not tape recorders recording the voice of God. This would indeed be contrary to the whole relationship between God and humankind in the Bible, to the first description of God as Liberator (Exodus), to what Paul tells us about the death of Jesus Christ, to the declaration "the truth sets you free," and finally, contrary to the resurrection—the liberation from death.

Freedom is the very essence of God's work in which mankind engages, as is shown in the Scriptures. In these circumstances, we do not see God or an "archangel" dictating the "message" verbatim. If, indeed, this were so, the Bible could not contain contradictions, which are the joy of the exegetes. In reality, the whole dynamic of the Bible, as it written, is this: God speaks to a person who receives this message, who understands it more or less, who interprets it, and who writes it down. I am well aware that I will shock the reader by saying that the biblical writer understood the message more or less, and yet that is so!

The prophets themselves acknowledge that they do not always understand the meaning of the message of which they are the bearers. Moreover, John's gospel seems to me to be the "Gospel of Misunderstandings." It is even John's will to highlight the misunderstandings between Jesus and those with whom he converses (Nicodemus, the Samaritan woman, and others). The Bible is not a dictated book; it is an "inspired" book. God *speaks* to a person and this person with their means, their limitations, their culture, is given the responsibility of translating this word of God and committing it to writing. Thus, even if the author is perfectly faithful, there is this essential transition from the word to paper. This implies the error in the (very Protestant) formula that states that the Bible is the "Word of God." On the contrary, it begins as a Word of God, and it can again become a Word of God, when the written text *speaks* anew and the Holy Spirit comes to seal this "re-enlivened" Word with the hallmark of truth! In other words, once again, the God of the Bible takes a human being as a partner, a partner to bear the truth that God has uttered, and which the person is responsible for writing down. Then this Word of God, mute as long as it remains enclosed in the pages of the book, revives when a person transforms anew the written document into spoken word and becomes the bearer of this truth (in speech, and in life!). Consequently, it is difficult to speak of two "religions of the Book" in order to reconcile Islam and Christianity.

The second radical difference between the two books appears to me even more fundamental, because it relates both to God and to his relationship with humankind. The Bible is above all, even almost exclusively, a book of history and stories. Of course, there are some books that are not: the Writings (Job, Ecclesiastes, Psalms) and Revelation. But the fact remains that even those are included within a story. Now this story, as with any historical account, is really a long sequence of events that have occurred, firstly to a people, Israel, then to a group of people, the disciples, who were to become the founders of the church. This story displays a remarkable peculiarity. It is a story of "God-with-man." It is obviously not a story of God "in whom there are neither variations nor changes" (and if there were we would know nothing about it!), but a story of the relationship between God and humans. This relationship is subject to significant "events," which occur because of humans, or because of God. The Bible traces a kind of pathway of God with humankind. That is, God lowers himself, from the outset, "down" to humans, to their level so as to be understood by them. He enters into dialogue with a person (even when he gives his "Commandments"); and he, the Transcendent One, cannot be fully grasped by humans; but he makes himself intelligible—hence the changes in his word, and in his decisions.

We do not always understand certain contradictions in the Bible, but they fit with God's having attuned himself to the people of a certain culture and a certain lifestyle. Critical historians understand nothing when they argue, for example, that certain textual passages can be explained because it is a question of nomads conceiving of a God for nomads. This is not the case. Rather God made sure that he could be understood *also* by the nomads. Indeed, we note that if it were not so, we would know *nothing* about God. There would be *no revelation* of God, simply because if God had revealed himself *without regard* to the one to whom he was speaking, he would be addressing humankind *in the abstract*, an essence of humankind, a theoretical model, which has never existed anywhere. In other words, a divine abstraction would "reveal" itself to a human abstraction. And I, a real human living today, I would not be much further on than before.

Yes, but can we say that God has stopped speaking; and therefore does his revelation to nomads, shepherds, warriors, and slaves, etc., still have anything to do with us? As some say, "God speaks no more to technological, globalised, literate humanity . . ." However, I am not sure that this objection is valid. In fact, to the extent that the word of God is addressed to a real person, I believe that the issues, muddles, and misfortunes of a real person today are not so different from those of a human 3,000 years ago. Do we have a more sophisticated intelligence? Yes, but this revelation of God is so extraordinary because it is not limited. It contains multiple meanings (which is not surprising if we consider it to be truly a *word* of God, and which is fascinating to us because it is multifaceted and especially multilayered in meaning). It takes this form because it was addressed to a person of that culture; but as the heirs, the successors, who have received this written word, knowing that it concerns us too, we have to search, starting from the meaning that it had for the shepherd, that it still has (the same, of course!) for the motorist! We must be careful however. I am not saying that people are identical from the Neanderthal to the present day, but only that the basic "accidents" of human life are the same today as 3,000 years ago. Between the misfortune suffered by the second-century slave and that of the miner in 1900, there is not a great distance! Between Roman decadence, without truth, without values, without "direction" in life, and the West today, the same is true.

This then is our work as conscientious recipients, to look beneath the obvious reading that says nothing to us, to what is the relevant kernel of truth for us! It is certainly a very difficult task, as it was for Moses to understand the words from the burning bush, for Elijah "left alone of all the faithful," and for Paul suddenly put into the most paradoxical situation.[1] However, what is marvelous in this text, and shows precisely to what extent God has put himself within our reach, is that in reading this Scripture,

---

1. This refers to the vision of Paul on the road to Damascus, which conferred on him the status of Apostle, in that he was an eyewitness of the life and resurrection of Christ.

the most ordinary, humble, or simple of people can also understand the truth therein. Experience has taught us this over and over again. The wisest realize that the more they advance in this knowledge, the more space God opens up before them, and the more God accompanies them in their personal and collective history. He is the God who so loves his creature, whom he formed in his own image and likeness, and whose happiness and misfortune he shares. God changes? Absolutely not! He is Everything. Rather, it is the relationship he establishes with humankind that changes. The ultimate point of this "God-with-man" adventure is obviously the incarnation of Jesus Christ, which is not a radically new event, but which takes this companionship to the extreme, to the point of a henceforth inseparable union. Moreover, one should not limit this presence of God to humanity, because he is present to the least creature, and is witness to all his creation.[2] Besides, insofar as we speak about love, we imply freedom, because there is no love under duress or by force; love assumes freedom and we can never interpret the commandments as "you must love . . .". God, the Free One *par excellence*, knows better than we do that love cannot be forced. The "commandment" "You shall love . . ." is certainly the introduction of a duty, but above all, it is a promise: the time will come when you will truly be able to love.

Again, we see the huge difference between the two books. In the Koran, where love is irrelevant, we have a duty and an unlimited constraint, with the punishment of hell. Islam means submission, and this submission is completely summed up in the Koran. Thus, the Judeo-Christian book is about a promise and openness to freedom; the Koran is about constraint and absolute certainty.

2. A passage that seems to me to show this wonderfully is the famous text on the "sparrow" generally translated incorrectly in Matthew 10:29. Jesus telling his followers to stop fearing, reminds them by saying of these small birds, "Do you not sell two sparrows for a penny? However, not one falls to the ground *without your Father*." It is often translated as "the will of your Father," which is not in the Greek and which changes the meaning. This addition means that the bird dies by the will of the Father. But the text means something else: no sparrow falls to earth without the Father's presence, without the Father accompanying it. It never dies alone; the Father is always present in the ordeal.

If in the Bible, Jesus Christ comes for us and for our salvation, once and for all; by contrast the Koranic revelation is once and for all, without possibility of review or hope of salvation (which is undeserved). Moreover, the divergence is all the greater when we reflect that in one case God spoke and from then on was silent; while in the other, God continues to reveal himself, and to speak to the believer and to his church, throughout its history. But there is nothing automatic either. God speaks in his freedom "at the level" he chooses and he can remain silent too. God's silence is significant and occurs sometimes in a way incomprehensible to humankind. In the beginning of the Book of Samuel the writer says, "The word of God was rare in those days" (1 Sam 3:1). In the Psalms it says, "We receive no more signs. There is no longer any prophet and there is no one among us who knows how long . . ." (Ps 74:9). And Amos says, "They shall run to and fro, looking for the Word of the Eternal, and they shall not find it" (Amos 8:12). However, God's silence is experienced as a drama in the *relationship* between God and humankind. This is not a mere observation; humans experience it as a rupture and a judgment. So, we are reimmersed in this story where "normal" is the exchange of prayer with the Father and the Word of the Almighty; but there is no established charter, no acquired stability. Therefore, one can perfectly know and receive a peace in this relationship, an infinitely sustainable and profound peace; but there is no security, no guarantee, and no establishment of ownership of a revealed God by the faithful. On the one hand, we have an unchangeable word, which generates an admirable poem. On the other hand, there is a story with its variations, at times "full of noise and fury," at others supernaturally peaceful. Here we meet the most commonplace as well as the most extraordinary. It is so extraordinary because, even before the incarnation, where we witness this apparent impossibility of God who comes to suffer as human, the Hebrew Bible shows that God suffers and is made to suffer by humankind. This is certainly unthinkable in the Koran and Islam. "I've stretched out my hands all day towards this rebellious people," God complains, "a people who say to me 'Keep to yourself . . .'" (Isa 65:2–5). And more moving still is this questioning, "My people, what have I done to you? In what have I wearied you?" (Mic 6:3). Thus, God is not immovable.

He is the one who constantly awaits a return to him, an impulse of love. And may it not be said that this is a case of coarse anthropomorphism. Those who think so have a very unbiblical idea of the eternal God, as impassive, sovereign, and judge, and forget the fact of the incarnation, of God's suffering. This is incomprehensible for Islam, because there is a world of difference between Allah the merciful and compassionate, and JHWH, who is no less sovereign, but who puts himself in the place of the one he has created, not to judge that person as is said in the Koran, but as his partner. They are mutually indispensable in their love. It is impossible for JHWH to even imagine being or doing without this one who represents his love. And the created one, whom God loved first and who is intended for love, loves as well, by virtue of his creation in God's image and likeness.

This is far from the idea of law or of a unilateral relationship between master and subject. Indeed Torah means teaching, and not constraint or obligation. The God of the Bible could also be called merciful, but this does not have the same meaning as in the Koran. There, God is the supreme Sovereign who concedes from up on high, in perfect arbitrariness, to show his mercy to the believer. In the Bible, God enters the life of the one to whom he is merciful in order to share his weakness and his pain. This is a God whose mercy is expressed, not in giving some superficial consolation, but in *sharing* the suffering, in order to be alongside the one who is suffering. Admittedly, in both cases God does not remove the suffering. But in one case, he allows it to go on, even if he does not cause it (that is the meaning of *Mektoub*[3]— it is the will of God, we can do nothing about it and there is no point in asking Allah to remove it), and the suffering of the believer apparently has no meaning. In the framework of the Christian revelation, it is quite different: suffering does not have just one source, it may be imposed by God, as in Islam, but it can also and more often come from evil forces, Satan (as in Job), or any evil force that takes hold

---

3. Normally translated as "fate" or "predestination"—*Translator.*

of the person. However, it is not primarily in this difference of origin that suffering is of a different order. In the Christian revelation, suffering *must* be received, either as punishment (the presence of hell among us), or as a test (intended to strengthen our faith), or as an appeal through the questioning that arises from it. God is never *for* suffering. Jesus, who came precisely to bear our suffering, so that we are never alone, presents both aspects. On the one hand, he heals and removes human suffering; on the other hand, he assumes this suffering as it is inevitable in the world's disorder and in the unleashing of the forces of evil. Nevertheless, it is important for the Christian to understand, in view of revelation, what *meaning* he can (or must) give to his suffering. The Christian is called to reflect on his suffering, not to submit to an arbitrary will of God. If God allows this ordeal, punishment, or calling, what does he wish to tell me? Here again, in asking us to participate in his plan for us, the relationship of the God of the Bible with us is flexible. So we see even better, the huge distance between a God calling for collaboration and the solitary sovereignty of Allah.

§

I will therefore conclude this short study, which could be more extensive, but would have the same results, by saying that there are similarities of *words* between the biblical revelation and Islam that hide the fundamental difference. In Islam, it is a question of God, the All Powerful, a God *alone*, creator, and spirit, with sin and judgment followed by a resurrection, all of which is contained in a revealed book. Therefore, the idea has arisen that all this closely approximates the biblical revelation. However, this is only because of the *words*, the meaning of which must be clarified, at which point we notice the impassable gulf between the two. The resemblance of the words completely hides the differences between the *meaning* and the *being*.

Part II

Other Essays
by Jacques Ellul on Islam

1

The Influence of Islam[1,2]

Stress has seldom been laid upon the influence of Islam on Christianity, that is, on the deformation and subversion to which God's revelation in Jesus Christ is subjected. Yet this influence was considerable between the ninth and eleventh centuries. We have been brought up on the image of a strong and stable Christianity that was attacked and besieged in some sense by Islam. Engaged in unlimited conquest, with a universal vocation similar to that claimed by Christianity, Islam was expanding its empire in three directions: to the south, especially along the coasts into black Africa, and reaching as far as Zanzibar by the twelfth century; to the northwest, with the conquest of Spain and the invasion of France up to Lyons on the one side and Poitiers on the other; and to the northeast into Asia Minor and as far as Constantinople. With the Turks, Islam would then continue incessantly to threaten the Balkans, Austria, Hungary, etc. The picture is a Manichean and warlike one; as it is hard to conceive of profound contacts between

---

1. Ellul, *The Subversion of Christianity,* chapter 5, 95–112.

2. Among other works on Islam, see Sourdel, *L'Islam médiéval,* and on Muslim mysticism Eliade, *Histoire des croyances,* 3:283; and Ellul, ed., "Islam et Christianisme."

warring enemies, how can Islam have influenced Christianity in this permanent state of *war*?

The fine book by H. Pirenne, *Mahomet et Charlemagne*, has admirably shown what were the economic and political consequences of this permanent military threat. But it has often been emphasized that we lack any study of relationships. This is the more surprising in that elsewhere, in the domain of philosophy, we know perfectly well that Aristotle's thought came into Europe thanks to the translations and commentaries of the Arab philosopher Averroes (twelfth century), and we can also point to the influence of Avicenna from the eleventh century. It is also recognized that Arab influence was great in scientific fields such as mathematics, medicine, agronomy, astronomy, and physics. All this is conceded and generally known.

A little later, Arab influence may be seen incontestably in the black arts, in magic, the various "–mancies," alchemy, the search for the philosopher's stone, and also music (twelfth century). It is also well understood that the Arabs had considerable military influence (e.g., upon cavalry, etc.) and that some technical fields (irrigation) and architecture felt their impact. Finally, it is constantly stressed that through the Crusades and the contacts of the Crusaders with the Arabs many changes came about in various areas, such as the bringing of certain fruit trees (cherries and apricots) into France. All this is very banal. But it does at least tell us beyond a doubt that even between enemies who are depicted as irreconcilable there were cultural and intellectual relations. Exchanges took place and knowledge circulated. In truth, knowledge seems to have circulated in only one direction, coming from Islam and the Arab world to the West, which was much more backward and "barbarian."[3]

3. This has led some fervent supporters of Islam to regret that the Arabs were finally defeated and repulsed. What a wonderfully civilized empire would have been set up if all Europe had been invaded! This position, the opposite of the prevailing one in history up to about 1950, leads people to forget the horrors of Islam, the dreadful cruelty, the general use of torture, the slavery, and the absolute intolerance notwithstanding zealous apostles who underline Islam's toleration. We shall come back to this. It is enough to point out that

There are two areas that to my knowledge have not yet been studied in such surveys, those of law and theology. But how can we believe or admit or think that exchanges took place in the intellectual, commercial, and economic fields without affecting these disciplines in any way? It is recognized, for example, that the bill of exchange was almost certainly invented by the Arabs and then adopted in the West to facilitate maritime trade. But other areas of law must have been influenced as well. I am inclined to think, for example, that the law of serfdom is a Western imitation of the Muslim *dhimmi*. Religious law is also important. I am convinced that some parts of canon law have their origin in Arab law. And this leads us, in effect, to Christianity.

How can we imagine that there was a well known admitted influence on philosophy that did not have theological repercussions? Everyone knows that the problem solved by Thomas Aquinas was precisely that of the confrontation between classical theology and Aristotle's philosophy. But the bridge is by way of the Arabs. We speak of Greek philosophy and Christian theology. But this Greek philosophy was faithfully transmitted by Arab interpreters. It was by way of Arab Muslim thinking that the problem came to be addressed at this time. We can hardly think that the Arab influence was nil except in matters concerning Aristotle.

Furthermore, it is readily perceived that Christianity and Islam had certain obvious points in common or points of meeting. Both were monotheistic and both were based on a book. We should also note the importance that Islam accords to the poor. Certainly Christians reject Allah because of the denial that Jesus Christ is God's Son, and they do not allow that the Koran is divinely inspired. On the other hand, Muslims reject the Trinity in the name of the unity, and they make the whole Bible a mere preface or introduction to the Koran. At root, Muslims do with the whole Bible what Christians do with the Hebrew Bible. But on this

wherever Islam gained a hold, strong and vital churches like those of North Africa and Asia Minor simply disappeared. And all native cultures that were different, that the Romans and Germans had respected, were exterminated in areas conquered by the Arabs.

common foundation there are necessarily encounters and debates and discussions, and hence a certain openness. Even where there is rejection and objection, there can be no evading the question that is put.

It seems that the Muslim intellectuals and theologians were much stronger than their Christian counterparts. It seems that Islam had an influence, but not Christianity. Our interest here is not in the philosophical problem or in theological formulations, which were necessarily restricted to a small intellectual circle, but in the way in which Islamic influences change practices, rites, beliefs, attitudes toward life, all that belongs to the domain of moral or social belief or conduct, all that constitutes Christendom. Here again, everyone knows that the Frankish kingdom of Jerusalem, the French knights installed in Palestine, rapidly adopted many manners and customs that originated in Islam. But the exceptional case is not important. What counts is what is imported into Europe. It is the fact of unwitting imitation. It is the fact of being situated on the chosen territory, and being delimited by those whom one wants to combat. I will thus leave on one side theology in the pure sense, the difference between Thomas Aquinas and biblical theology, and the influence of Aristotle. I will concern myself with other problems.

I believe that in every respect the spirit of Islam is contrary to that of the revelation of God in Jesus Christ. It is so in the basic fact that the God of Islam cannot be incarnate. This God can be only the sovereign judge who ordains all things as he wills. Another point of antithesis lies in the absolute integration of religious and political law. The expression of God's will inevitably translates itself into law. No law is not religious, inspired by God. Reciprocally, all God's will must translate itself into legal terms. Islam pushed to an extreme a tendency that is virtual in the Hebrew Bible, but there it is symbolic of the spiritual and is then transcended by Jesus Christ; with Islam we come back to legal formulation as such.

I have shown elsewhere that the twofold formulation of "having a law" and of "objective law" is contrary to revelation. This can naturally be contested only by champions of natural law and classical theology. My conviction is that this revelation of love, seeking to set up a relationship of love (alone) among us, and thus basing everything on grace and giving us a model of exclusively gracious relationships, is in fact the exact opposite of law, in which everything is measured by debits and credits (the opposite of grace) and duties (the opposite of love).

To the extent that we are not in the kingdom of God, we certainly cannot achieve this pure relation of love and grace, this completely transparent relation. Hence law has a necessary existence. Yet we have to view it merely as a matter of expediency (because we cannot do better) and a necessary evil (which is always an evil). This understanding has nothing in common with that which contrariwise greatly exalts law, making it the expression of God's will and the legal formulation of the "religious" world. On this view law is a preeminent value. In taking this approach Christians were greatly influenced by their Roman background. They could not exclude or minimize the value of Roman law, as we have seen. There then comes a great rebound with the Arabs. We now have an intimate union between law and the will of God.

The jurist is the theologian. Theology becomes no less legal than philosophical. Life is set in law no less and even more than in ethics. Everything religious becomes legal. Judges handle religious matters, and jurisprudence becomes theology. This gives an enormous boost to the juridicizing of Christendom. Canon law expands after the pattern found in Islam. If everything is not included in it, it is because the feudal lords and monarchs are very hostile to the growing power of the church and because (lay) customs put up firm opposition to this sanctification. But the legal spirit penetrates deeply into the church, and I maintain that this is both under the influence of Islam and in *response* to the religious law of Islam. The church had to follow suit.

Furthermore, law set up ecclesiastical courts and gave them means of ruling. They would have liked to have seen everything referred to canon law and their courts, as in the Muslim world. The church would have liked sole power. But in Islam there was an indissoluble correlation between religious law and political power.

In this field, too, what was introduced with Constantinianism, as we have seen, received a new impulse from Islam. Every political head in Islam is also the ruler of believers. There is no separation between the church and political power. The political head is the religious head. He is a representative of Allah. His political and military acts, etc., are inspired.

Now this is all familiar in Europe. The king or emperor does not merely claim to be the secular arm of the church but the one who has spiritual power. He wants it to be recognized that he personally is chosen by God, elected by the Almighty. He needs a prophetic word and the power to work miracles. His word and person have to be sacred.

Naturally some of this was already present prior to Islam. It was not for nothing, however, that this theology, liturgy, and imperial understanding developed first at Byzantium on the first contact with Islam, and only later spread to the West. Royal power becomes religious not merely in an alliance with the church but under the influence of Islam, which was much more of a theocracy than the West ever was: a theocracy in which God is indeed the sole king, but the true representative of God on earth is the political head, so that we have what has rightly been called "lay theocracy" with no religious organization, no clergy, no ecclesiastical institution—a situation in which to rejoice, for it implies that only the political power is religious. Islam does not know the duality of church and state with its conflicts and also with the limitation that it entails for the political power.

We can thus understand perfectly the wish or desire or temptation of Western kings and emperors to be themselves the sole representatives of God on earth and thus to go much further than Constantine. The formula according to which the emperor is "the bishop on the outside" did not suffice for them. I am certain that the Islamic model acted in favor of the emancipation of kings and their attempt from the fourteenth century to create a church that would be wholly dependent on the political power. Certainly in the big debate they were not able to advance this argument. What an admission it would be to say that they were taking those terrible unbelievers as a model!

In tandem with this great importance of the political power there is, of course, the importance and glorification of war as a means of spreading the faith. Such war is a duty for all Muslims. Islam has to become universal. The true faith, not the power, has to be taken to every people by every means, including by military force. This makes the political power important, for it is warlike by nature. The two things are closely related. The political head wages war on behalf of the faith. He is thus the religious head, and as the sole representative of God he must fight to extend Islam. This enormous importance of war has been totally obliterated today in intellectual circles that admire Islam and want to take it afresh as a model. War is inherent in Islam. It is inscribed in its teaching. It is a fact of its civilization and also a religious fact; the two cannot be separated. It is coherent with its conception of the *dhar al-harb*, that the whole world is destined to become Muslim by Arab conquests. The proof of all this is not just theological; it is historical: hardly has the Islamic faith been preached when an immediate military conquest begins. From 632 to 651, in the twenty years after the death of the prophet, we have a lightning war of conquest with the invasion of Egypt and Cyrenaica to the west, Arabia in the center, and Armenia, Syria, and Persia to the east. In the following century all of North Africa and Spain are taken over, along with India and Turkey to the east. The conquests are not achieved by sanctity, but by war.

For three centuries Christianity spread by preaching, kindness, example, morality, and encouragement of the poor. When the empire became Christian, war was hardly tolerated by the Christians. Even when waged by a Christian emperor it was a dubious business and was assessed unfavorably. It was often condemned. Christians were accused of undermining the political force and military might of the empire from within. In practice Christians would remain critical of war until the flamboyant image of the holy war came on the scene. In other words, no matter what atrocities have been committed in wars waged by so-called

Christian nations, war has always been in essential contradiction to the gospel. Christians have always been more or less aware of this. They have judged war and questioned it.

In Islam, on the contrary, war was always just and constituted a sacred duty. The war that was meant to convert infidels was just and legitimate, for, as Muslim thinking repeats, Islam is the only religion that conforms perfectly to nature. In a natural state we would all be Muslims. If we are not, it is because we have been led astray and diverted from the true faith. In making war to force people to become Muslims the faithful are bringing them back to their true nature. QED. Furthermore, a war of this kind is a *jihad*, a holy war. Let us make no mistake; the word "jihad" has two complementary senses. It may denote a spiritual war that is moral and inward. Muslims have to wage this war within themselves in the fight against demons and evil forces, in the effort to achieve better obedience to God's will, in the struggle for perfect submission. But at the same time and in a wholly consistent way the jihad is also the war against external demons. To spread the faith, it is necessary to destroy false religions. This war, then, is *always* a religious war, a *holy war.*

At this point we have two very strong direct influences exerted by Islam on Christianity. Prior to the eighth century Christianity hardly ever stated that revelation conforms to nature. Tradition, based on the Bible, took the contrary view. Nature is fallen, the flesh is wicked, people in themselves, in their natural state, are sinners and unbelievers. Naturally I realize that the church fathers had already run into the problem of the contradiction between the biblical statements and, for example, Greek philosophy, which in certain streams presents nature as the model that one should follow. But nature was never confused with the biblical revelation. Even those who allowed some positive value to nature always had reservations about corrupted nature. I believe that it is the Muslim identification of nature and Islam that poses for Christians in an urgent way the question of whether one could let infidels get away with this, whether one had not to say something similar.

As is well known, theologies from the eleventh century onward tend to bring nature and revelation together, to find in nature a source of revelation (as in the ambiguous statements of Denis about light), to elaborate a "natural" theology, to show that the fall is not radical or total, and then to coordinate the two in a nature completed by grace as supernature. Thus the great deviation of Christian thought and theology from the biblical revelation in this matter of nature has at least two sources: the Greek and the Arab. The latter, in my opinion, is finally the more important. This orientation leads at once to the same conclusions we have noted in Islam. If there is a coincidence of nature and revelation, then only damnable blindness leads to the nonrecognition of God (the Christian God, of course!). For one has only to open one's eyes and look at nature to see God. One has only to know oneself to discern the true religion. If one will not do such simple things, one is culpable. As soon as Christianity becomes a religion that conforms to nature, then it becomes necessary to force people to become Christians. In this way they will come back to their true nature. Forced conversions begin to take place.

The famous story of Charlemagne forcing the Saxons to be converted on pain of death simply presents us with an imitation of what Islam had been doing for two centuries. But if war now has conversions to Christianity as its goal, we can see that very quickly it takes on the aspect of a holy war. It is a war waged against unbelievers and heretics (we know how pitiless was the war that Islam waged against heretics in its midst). But the idea of a holy war is a direct product of the Muslim jihad. If the latter is a holy war, then obviously the fight against Muslims to defend or save Christianity has *also* to be a holy war. The idea of a holy war is not of Christian origin. Emperors never advanced the idea prior to the appearance of Islam.

For half a century historians have been studying the Crusades to find explanations other than the silly theory that was previously held and conforms to addresses and sermons, that claims their intention was to secure the holy places. It has been shown that the Crusades had economic objectives, or that they were stirred up by the popes for various political motives such as that of securing papal preeminence by exhausting the kingdoms, or reforging the weakening unity of the church, or again that they were a means whereby the kings ruined the barons who were challenging their power, or again that the bankers of Genoa, Florence, and Barcelona instigated them so as to be able to lend money to the Crusaders and make fabulous profits, etc. One fact, however, is a radical one, namely, that the Crusade is an imitation of the *jihad.* Thus the Crusade includes a guarantee of salvation. The one who dies in a holy war goes straight to Paradise, and the same applies to the one who takes part in a Crusade. This is no coincidence; it is an exact equivalent.

The Crusades, which were once admired as an expression of absolute faith, and which are now the subject of accusations against the church and Christianity, are of Muslim, not Christian, origin. We find here a terrible consequence and confirmation of a vice that was eating into Christianity already, namely, that of violence and the desire for power and domination. To fight against a wicked foe with the same means and arms is unavoidably to be identified with this foe. Evil means inevitably corrupt a just cause. The nonviolence of Jesus Christ changes into a war in conflict with that waged by the foe. Like that war, this is now a holy war. Here we have one of the chief perversions of faith in Jesus Christ and of the Christian life.

But we must take this a step further. Once the king is the representative of God on earth and a war is holy, another question necessarily arises. If a war is not holy, what is it? It seems that the Christian emperors of Rome did not ask this question. They had to defend the empire. That was all. Naturally it did not arise in the period of the invasions and the Germanic kingdoms either. War was then a fact, a permanent state. No one tried to justify it. But with the Muslim idea of a holy war the idea is born that a war may be good even if it is not motivated by religious intentions so long as it is waged by a legitimate king. Gradually the view is accepted that political power has to engage in war, and if this power is Christian, then a ruler has to obey certain precepts, orientations, and criteria if he is to act as a Christian ruler and to wage a just war. We thus embark on an endless debate as to the conditions of a just war, from Gratian's decree to St. Thomas. All this derives from the first impulse toward a holy war, and it was the Muslim example that finally inspired this dreadful denial of which all Christendom becomes guilty.

We have still to examine a very different subversion. It concerns piety, the relation to God. We see in it an influence that we have already mentioned in passing. Every infant is supposedly born a Muslim, for Islam is perfect conformity to nature. Scholars, then, argue that it is through a bad influence or the "cultural" setting that this baby, who is by nature a Muslim, deviates from the truth and becomes a Jew, a Christian, or a pagan. Evangelical thinking takes exactly the opposite view. One becomes a Christian only by conversion. Our old being, which is by nature corrupt, is changed by the action of the Holy Spirit, who makes of us new beings. Conversion alone, conscious and recognized, so that there is confession with the lips as well as faith in the heart, produces the Christian. This new birth, the opposite of natural birth, is confirmed by the outward sign of baptism, which seems to imply an express acknowledgment of faith. But progressively this strict view weakens. The church fathers analyze the sacraments, and the tendency toward an opus operatum understanding develops. The sacrament is intrinsically efficacious. Baptism ceases to be a sign of converting grace and becomes in itself an instrument of salvation. Hence, if we desire that infants, who are naturally damned due to the transmission of original sin, should be saved, we must baptize them immediately at birth so as to avoid the risk of their dying first. Salvation, then, comes almost at the moment of birth. At the same time that we reevaluate nature, which is now not radically bad, the conviction gains ground that the soul is "naturally" good and saved, that there is only a hindrance, a flaw, and that original sin is merely an obstacle that baptism overcomes.

Very quickly the formula spreads that the soul is by nature Christian, which is the counterpart of the Muslim view. Now the idea that faith is natural, that one is put in a Christian state by heredity, that being a Christian is indeed a kind of status in society, that it involves at the same time membership in both the church and society (just as excommunication is exclusion from both the church and society), is the very opposite of the work of Jesus Christ. We have to insist that Christendom in this sense is superimposed upon the church, and that it duplicates exactly what is taught by Islam. Once the theory of "the soul by nature Christian" is accepted, society has to be made up of Christians. There is no alternative. Already with the Christian emperors there was a thrust in this direction. But it was the Muslim example that proved decisive. Each time we find the same refrain. There is a need to outdo Islam, and that means imitating it.

Now we have to say that this is the very opposite of what may be seen in the Gospels and in Paul. It negates the unique redemptive worth of the death of Jesus Christ. If human nature is not totally incapable of having access to God, if it is naturally in harmony with the will of God, what is the point of the death of Jesus Christ? It was not at all necessary that God should come among us, that Jesus should obey his Father's will even to the point of accepting death by reason of the evil that holds sway in the human race. The impossibility of our being able to be in harmony with God is shown by the fact that we reject the holy and the good, love and truth, in the person of Jesus. Unwittingly the imitation of Islam robs the death of Jesus Christ of its ultimate seriousness.

In this field of the relation to God, Christianity discloses the influence of Islam at two other points as well: mysticism and obedience. Mysticism is not essentially Christian. I would even say that in its final form it is more anti-Christian. I know that this will cause pain and anger in some circles. Yet when I look at the Bible I find hardly any examples of mystics. Paul alludes to his own experience; he knew a man who was lifted up to the third[4] heaven, and he could not say whether this was with or without the body. But he was not intentionally seeking union with God. He did not engage in a movement of ascent. He was caught up or taken up by an external force like the chariot of fire that catches up Elijah or the

4. Ellul mistakenly has "seventh" —*Geoffrey W. Bromiley (translator).*

hand of God that lifts up Daniel. Nothing more. We find prophets in the Old Testament and apostles in the New. In the enumeration of spiritual gifts there is no mention of mystical gifts. We are told to imitate Jesus Christ but not to achieve union with God by a mystical ascent.

When the apostles are invested with spiritual power, it is by tongues of flame that come down from heaven. There is no question of union with God. Jesus alone is in total union with God. Such union is brought about by the fact that God comes (down) to us, not by our spiritual intensity or psychological action or by any attempt to climb up to him. The idea of a possible union with God is ruled out by the revelation of cherubim guarding against any return to Paradise. As I have often said, there is no possible ascent to God, or access to him. But this is what mystics passionately seek. They want union with God. They have a discipline. They follow a path to the inner void where the soul is filled by the Holy Spirit and access opens up to God. This is the exact opposite of what the Bible teaches.

The antithesis is even more radical if one accepts the common etymology whereby "mystic" comes from *muein,* to be mute or speechless. How can this be when God's work is wholly that of the Word? God himself speaks, and he calls upon us to bear witness by the Word. There could hardly be a greater contradiction. In fact all mystical experiences are ineffable, and Paul is totally against anything of this kind. If we follow Jesus, it is not a matter of looking up to heaven ("Why do you look up to heaven?" etc.) but of being on earth and concretely living out the will of God that was done in Jesus Christ.

But mysticism is a fundamental aspect of the Muslim religion. There is undoubtedly some correlation with the Orient here. We know to what extent people seek ecstatic and mystical phenomena, using drugs and somatic techniques to achieve this abstract knowledge, this fusion with God. Fasts, exhausting dances, absolute silence, hashish, etc.—all things are good that lead to merger with God. Great Muslim mystics abound. Once again, prior to the relation with Islam, one may perceive certain mystical tendencies in Christianity, especially the trend that derives from Gnosticism and Neoplatonism. But this trend was regarded with suspicion and did not form any glorious part of the Christian life or the church. In contrast, mysticism is directly linked with Islam; it forms part of its spiritual development. Let us make no mistake; when I speak about the desire to mount up to God, this does not mean pride and conquest, for mystics view themselves as objects that are annihilated in God. But here again the biblical orientation is very different. Furthermore, I am not saying that the influence of Islam is the only one in this regard. My point is that it was *decisive* in the development of mysticism as an expression of Christian faith.

The second aspect seems to me to be the essential one, and it is not at all alien to the first. Islam means submission (to God's will). Just as mystics negate themselves to give place to God, so Muslims have the same religious orientation. Not just obedience but submission is involved. At a first glance this seems to be in full conformity with the biblical revelation. We know how important a role is played in current piety by the formula *mektoub,* it was written. We have to submit to the sovereign, preexistent, eternal, and immutable will of God. All history, all the events of history, all the things that come to pass in each individual life have already been decreed and fixed in advance and written by God. In reality this is the very reverse of what we are told about the biblical God, who opens up freedom for us, who lets us make our own history, who goes with us on the more or less unheard-of adventures that we concoct. This God is not "providence" (which is never a biblical word). He is never a determinative cause or an irreducible conductor of events. The biblical God is he who unceasingly reestablishes our human liberty when we keep falling into bondage. He unceasingly enters into dialogue with us, but only so as to warn us about what is good, to set us on guard, to associate us with his will; never to force us. Here again the tendency to believe in a God who because he is omnipotent is also omniscient (which presupposes that everything is already said) was already present in Christian thinking when it was invaded by certain elements in Greek thought. Yet at first, the themes of salvation and love were always dominant.

I believe that it was the strictness of Muslim piety that really led Christians along this path.

If we make God's omnipotence dominant over his love and autonomy, his transcendence over the incarnation and liberation, then we think of his omniscience as an inscribing of history and events in a nexus of events that has already been established, that is unchangeable and immutable, and that all takes place at a stroke. Then we do not have to enter into a dialogue with God, or into a monologue that, like Job's, demands a response from God, but simply have to submit to the unchanging and, in a true sense, inhuman will of God. The whole Bible, whether in the Old Testament or the Gospels, tells us that there is no such thing as destiny or fate. All this is replaced by love, and hence the joyful freedom that the first Christians experienced. But gradually, and insidiously, fate stages a comeback.

I admit that here again popular beliefs perpetuated the Roman idea of *fatum,* and that the idea of liberation from destiny had hard work making its way. I also admit that philosophical thought inclined theologians toward problems of this type: If God is omnipotent, it is he who *does* all things (cf. the error in translating Matt 10:29), he is not just the *causa sui* but the cause of causes . . . and the future as well as the past is before him. Hence our future is already there for God. We live out nothing, construct nothing, and can change nothing. It must be understood, however, that these are logical questions that have nothing whatever to do with what the Bible reveals to us. This logic tends to assimilate the biblical God to Roman ideas of God. To unite the relics of popular belief and philosophical deductions only some new input was needed, and I think that Islam supplied this with its specific conception of the omnipotent God who retains only one aspect of the Hebrew God and absolutizes it.

From now on destiny and divine omniscience are conjoined. Believers can live in perfect peace because they know that everything was written in advance and they can change nothing. The very formula "It was written" could come only from a religion of the book. Yet the Hebrew Bible and the Gospels never use such a formula. Thanks to it, the idea of predestination that was already haunting philosophical and Christian thinking received confirmation, forcibly established itself, and came to include double predestination (in Calvin), which, whether we want it or not, transforms the biblical God into destiny, Ananke, etc. And this derives from Muslim thinking. For it is not just historical events that were written in advance; it is also eternal salvation (or rejection). Ultimately this conviction came to dominate a good part of Christendom, and paganism rejoins it with its belief in the god of fate.

Finally, we have to take into account some rather different contributions of Islam, not directly in the theological field but with reference to some social implications of belief that are at every point inconsistent with Christian ethics. We have already met one of these: the holy war. A second on which I shall not expand, having studied it already, is the status of women. Another difficulty that arises in Islam in this regard is that modern Muslims claim that women are in every way equal to men and completely free, that Islam has been a movement of feminine emancipation. Yet one can go so far as to say that nowhere have women been more fully subject than on Muslim territory.[5] Marriages are arranged for young girls, women are reduced to being the slaves of men in poor families and are put in the harems of the wealthy; women have no rights, having no property—all this is beyond dispute. Furthermore, the well-known question whether women have souls (the church has run into trouble for asking this question, and some have wrongly alleged that in the eleventh and twelfth centuries it said women had no souls) is a question that was in reality posed by *Muslim theologians*. Before Arab theologians raised the issue, no one in the Christian world had any doubts about the matter. Indeed, in spite of the anti-Christian fable that is spread abroad with such satisfaction, the famous Council of Mâcon in particular (585 AD), to which reference is often made, did not deal with the matter, as H. Leclercq has shown incontrovertibly in his article in the

---

5. Cf. the fine study by Bousquet, *L'Éthique sexuelle de l'Islam* [*Sexual Ethics in Islam*]. The prophet's own practice was also not particularly edifying for women, and Muslims are told to copy him in all things.

Dictionnaire d'archéologie chrétienne (5:1349). The polemical legend rests solely on some misunderstood lines of Gregory of Tours on the subject, in which the question is a purely grammatical one, namely, whether the word *homo* is a generic term that may also apply to women (the answer being in the affirmative), and not a theological one, whether women are human beings furnished with souls. Neither Christianity nor the church ever denied that women have souls. Furthermore, it was certainly only in those Western lands subject to Muslim domination that the position of women deteriorated. A detailed study is impossible, but an answer to the question would have to be along the lines that I have indicated.

I have to admit that Christian history took an incredibly sad turn in two other areas. The first concerns slavery. Not all at once but progressively under Christian influence (and not because of technical improvements, as is often stated today), slavery disappeared in the Roman Empire. It persisted, however, in remote comers of the Carolingian empire. We may note, meanwhile, two currents: the one from the North (the Slavs), the other from the Mediterranean. Yet the incidence of this is negligible and episodic. The general thesis that there was no more slavery in Christendom is true. Thus the proclamation that "everyone in the kingdom of France is free" was correct, and it was even allowed (although perhaps theoretically) that the moment slaves arrived in France, the mere fact of setting foot on French soil made them free. This was wholly in keeping with Christian thinking.

Nevertheless, from the fifteenth century, with the development of a knowledge of Africa, and then especially in the seventeenth and eighteenth centuries, we have the familiar and dreadful history of the enslaving of Africans, who were torn from their own country and transported to America. What accusations have been made against "Christianity" and Western civilization! And rightly so! How lightly the revelation in Christ was taken, which would have totally, radically, and unreservedly forbidden slavery. In the Middle Ages the traffic in slaves would undoubtedly have led to excommunication. It is a curious fact, however, that apart from some conscientious historians no one has put the elementary question how it was that a few Western navigators could round up thousands of slaves from among peoples who were by no means sheeplike. Could a hundred French sailors, even though armed with muskets, attack a tribe of several hundred hardy warriors and seize a cargo of slaves? Such an idea is pure fiction. For centuries the Muslims had regularly cropped the black continent for slaves. Seizing Africans as slaves was a Muslim practice from at least the tenth century. The African tribes were in this case attacked by considerable armies, in veritable invasions, of which we shall have to speak later.[6]

The Muslims carried off to the East far more black slaves than the Westerners ever did. In the eleventh century fifteen great slave markets were set up by the Arabs in black Africa. In the east they extended as far as across from Madagascar [present-day Mozambique], and in the west as far as the Niger [present-day Guinea River]. Slaves were the main item in Muslim trade from the tenth century to the fifteenth. Furthermore, the Muslims began to use political methods by which the Western merchants profited. They played off the African chiefs against one another in such a way that a chief would take prisoners from neighboring tribes and then sell them to the Arab merchants. It was by following this practice, which had been established for many centuries, that the Western sailors obtained slaves so easily. Naturally, the reality itself is terrible and anti-Christian, but we see here the direct influence of Islam on the practice of Westerners who were Christian only in name. One should also remember, as the United Nations has pointed out, that trading in black slaves by Arab merchants still goes on in countries around the gulf of Oman.

Finally, a last point: colonizing. Here again, for the last thirty years some have attacked Christianity for instigating colonialism. Christians are accused of invading the whole world and justifying the capitalist system. It has become a traditional belief that missionaries pioneered the way for merchants. Undoubtedly there

---

6. Apart from the wars, we also find brutal expeditions that were mounted solely to seize prisoners as slaves or to carry off herds and women. For these the word is *razzia*, a good Arab term.

is some truth in all this. Undoubtedly serious and conscientious Christians should never have acquiesced in the invasion of "Third World" peoples, in the seizing of their lands, in their reduction to semi-slavery (or their extermination), in the destruction of their cultures. The judgment against us is a crushing one. Las Casas is entirely right. But who invented colonizing? Islam. Incontestably so!

I will not discuss again the question of war or the establishment in Africa of kingdoms dominated by the Arabs. My theme is colonizing, the penetration by other than military means, the reduction of subject peoples by a sort of treaty that makes them do exactly as the rulers want. In Islam we find two methods of penetration, commercial and religious. Things are exactly the same as they will be among the Westerners five centuries later. Muslim missionaries convert the Africans to Islam by every possible means. Nor can one deny that their intervention has just the same effects as that of Christian missionaries: the destruction of the independent religions and cultures of the African tribes and kingdoms. Nor must we back the stupid argument that it was an internal affair of the African world. The Muslims came into the north by conquest, and the Arabs are white. Muslim missionaries went as far as Zanzibar, and in Angola they brought within the Muslim orbit African peoples that had not been conquered or subjugated.

The other method is that of commerce. The Arab merchants go much further afield than the soldiers. They do much the same as the Westerners will do five centuries later. They set up trading posts and barter with the local tribes. It is not without interest that one of the commodities they were seeking in the tenth and eleventh centuries was gold. Trading in gold by the Arabs took place in Ghana, to the south of the Niger, and on the east coast down toward Zanzibar. When it is said that the desire for gold prompted the Westerners in the fifteenth century, they were simply following in the footsteps of Islam. Thus the Arab mechanism of colonizing serves as a model for the Europeans.

In conclusion, let me make it clear that I have not been trying to excuse what the Europeans did. I have not been trying to shift the "blame," to say that the Muslims, not the Christians, were the guilty party. My purpose is to try to explain certain perversions in Christian conduct. I have found a model for them in Islam. Christians did not invent the holy war or the slave trade. Their great fault was to imitate Islam. Sometimes this was direct imitation by following the example of Islam. Sometimes it was inverse imitation by doing the same thing in order to combat Islam, as in the Crusades. Either way, the tragedy was that the church completely forgot the truth of the gospel. It turned Christian ethics upside down in favor of what seemed to be very obviously a much more effective mode of action, for in the twelfth century and later the Muslim world offered a dazzling example of civilization. The church forgot the authenticity of the revelation in Christ in order to launch out in pursuit of the same mirage.

2

Preface to *The Dhimmi*[1]

This is a very important book, for it deals with one of the most sensitive problems of our time, sensitive owing to the difficulty of the subject—the reality of Islamic doctrine and practice with regard to non-Muslims, and sensitive owing to the topicality of the subject and the susceptibilities it now arouses throughout the world. Half a century ago the question of the condition of non-Muslims in the Islamic countries would not have excited anyone. It might have been the subject of a historical dissertation of interest to specialists, the subject of a juridical analysis (I am thinking of the work of M. Gaudefroy-Demombynes, and of my old colleague G.-H. Bousquet, who wrote extensively on different aspects of Muslim law and history without their research giving rise to the smallest controversy), or the subject of a philosophical and theological discussion, but without passion. That which was related to Islam and the Muslim world was believed to belong to a past that, if not dead, was certainly no more alive than medieval Christianity. The Muslim peoples had no power; they were extraordinarily di-

1. Text written by Jacques Ellul in May 1983 as the preface to Bat Ye'or, *The Dhimmi*. This text—published in editions in English, Hebrew, and Russian—was never previously published in French.

[This preface is reproduced here in the English version with permission —*Translator*.]

vided, and many of them were subjected to European colonization. Those Europeans who were hostile to colonization showed some sympathy for the "Arabs," but that was as far as it went! And then suddenly, since 1950, everything changed completely. I think that one can discern four stages in this development. The first was the attempt of the Islamic peoples to rid themselves of their conquerors. In this, the Muslims were by no means "original": the Algerian war and all that followed was only a consequence of the first war against the French in Vietnam. It was part of a general process of decolonization. This process, in turn, led the Islamic people to search for their own identity, to seek to be not only free of the Europeans, but different, qualitatively different from them. This led to the second step: that which was specific to these peoples was not an ethnic or organizational peculiarity, but a religion. Accordingly, even in left-wing socialist or communist movements, in the Muslim world, there was a return to religion, so that the idea of a secular state, such as Atatürk, for instance, had envisaged, was completely rejected. The explosion of Islamic religiosity is frequently considered specific to the Ayatollah Khomeini, but that is not correct. One ought not to forget that the terrible war of 1947 in India between the Muslims and Hindus was fought on a purely religious basis. More than one million people died, and since massacres had not taken place when the Muslims had lived within the Hindu-Buddhist orbit, one may presume that the war was caused by the attempt to set up an independent Islamic republic. Pakistan officially proclaimed itself an Islamic republic in 1953, precisely at a time when other Muslim peoples were making their great effort to regain their identity. Hardly a year has since passed without its marking some new stage in the religious revival of Islam (e.g., the resumption of the conversion of Black Africa to Islam, the return of alienated populations to religious practice, the obligation for Arab socialist regimes to proclaim that their states were "Muslim" republics, etc.), so that at the present day Islam can be said to be the most active religion in the world. The extremism of the Ayatollah Khomeini can be understood only in the light of this general tendency. It is not something exceptional and extraordinary, but its logical continuation. But, together with this religious renewal, there arose an awareness of a certain unity of the Islamic world over and above its political and cultural diversity. This was the third stage in the Islamic revival. Of course, one ought not to overlook all the conflicts between Muslim states, their divergences of interests and even wars, but these differences should not blind us to a more fundamental reality: their religious unity in opposition to the non-Muslim world. And here we have an interesting phenomenon: I would be tempted to say that it is the "others," the "communist" and "Christian" countries, that reinforce unity of the Muslim world, playing, as it were, the role of a "compressor," to bring about its unification. Finally, and this is obviously the last stage, there was the discovery of Islam's oil resources and economic power, which hardly needs elaboration. Taken as a whole, this process follows a logical sequence: political independence, religious revival, and economic power. It has transformed the face of the world in less than half a century. And we are now witnessing a vast program to propagate Islam, involving the building of mosques everywhere (even in the USSR), the diffusion of Arab literature and culture, and the recovery of a history. Islam now boasts of having been the cradle of all civilizations at a time when Europe was sunk in barbarism and the Far East was torn asunder by divisions. Islam as the origin of all the sciences and arts is a theme that is constantly developed. This idea has perhaps been promoted more in France than in the English-speaking world (although one should not forget the black Muslims in the United States). If I take the French situation as my yardstick, it is because I feel that it can serve as an example.

The moment one broaches a problem relating to Islam, one touches upon a subject where strong feelings are easily aroused. In France, it is not acceptable to criticize Islam or the Arab countries. There are several reasons for this: the French have a guilty conscience on account of their invasion and colonization of North Africa, doubly so after the Algerian War (which, by a backlash, has brought about a climate of sympathy for the adversary), and then there has also been the discovery of the fact, true enough, that for centuries Western culture has underestimated the value of the Muslim contribution to civilization (and, as a result, now goes to the other extreme). The flow of immigrant workers of Arab origin into France has established an important group that is generally wretched and despised (with racial overtones). This has led many intellectuals, Christians and others, to be favorably and uncritically disposed towards them. A general rehabilitation of Islam has therefore taken place that has been expressed in two ways. On the intellectual level there is first of all an increasing number of works of an apparently scholarly nature whose declared purpose is to eradicate prejudices and false preconceptions about Islam, with regard to both its doctrines and its customs. Thus these works "demonstrate" that it is untrue that the Arabs were cruel conquerors and that they disseminated terror and massacred those peoples who would not submit to their rule. It is false that Islam is intolerant; on the contrary, it is held to be tolerance itself. It is false that women had an inferior status and that they were excluded from public life. It is false that jihad (holy war) was a war fought for material gain, and so on. In other words, everything that has been regarded as historically unquestionable about Islam is considered as propaganda, and a false picture of Islam has been implanted in the West, which, it is claimed, must be corrected by the truth. Reference is made to a very spiritual interpretation of the Koran, and the excellence of the manners and customs in Islamic countries is emphasized.

But this is not all. In some Western European countries, Islam exerts a special spiritual fascination. Inasmuch as Christianity no longer possesses the religious influence it once had and is strongly criticized, and communism has lost its prestige and is no longer regarded as being the bearer of a message of hope, the religious needs of Europeans require another form in which to find expression, and Islam has been rediscovered. It is no longer a matter of exchange of ideas between intellectuals, but rather of an authentic religious adherence. Several well-known French intellectuals made a spectacular conversion to Islam. Islam is presented as a very great advance over Christianity, and reference is made to

Muslim mystics. It is recalled that the three religions of the book (Jewish, Christian, and Muslim) are all related. All of them claim Abraham as their ancestor, and the last one, the most recent, must obviously be the most advanced of the three. I am not exaggerating. Among Jews in France there are even serious intellectuals who hope, if not for a fusion, at least for a coming together of the three religions. If I have described what may be observed in Europe, it is because—whether one likes it or not—Islam regards itself as having a universal vocation and proclaims itself to be the only religion to which everyone must adhere. We should have no illusions about the matter: no part of the world will be excluded. Now that Islam has national, military, and economic power, it will attempt to extend its religion everywhere, including the British Commonwealth and the United States. In the face of this expansion (for the third time), one should not react by racism, nor by orthodox dogmatism, nor by persecution or war. The reaction should be of a spiritual and psychological nature (one must avoid being carried away by a guilty conscience), and on a scholarly level. What really happened? What was the reality: the cruelties of the Muslim conquest or the magnanimity and beneficence of the Koran? What is correct as regards doctrine and its application to daily life in the Muslim world? And the search that is done must be intellectually serious, *relating to specific points*. It is impossible to judge the Islamic world in a general way: a hundred different cultures have been absorbed by Islam. It is impossible to study all the doctrines, all the traditions and their applications together. Such a study can only be undertaken if one limits oneself to the study of specific questions, disentangling what is true from what is false.

It is within this context that Bat Ye'or's book, *The Dhimmi*, should be placed: and it is an exemplary contribution to this crucial discussion that concerns us all. Here I shall neither give an account of the book nor praise its merits, but shall simply indicate its importance. The *dhimmi* is someone who lives in a Muslim society without being a Muslim (Jews, Christians, and occasionally "animists"). He has a particular social, political, and economic status, and it is essential for us to know how this "refractory" person has been treated. But first of all, one ought to realize the dimensions of this subject: it is much more than the study of one "social condition" among others. The reader will see that, in many ways, the dhimmi was comparable to a European serf of the Middle Ages. But the condition of serfdom was the result of certain historic changes such as the transformation of slavery, the end of the state, the emergence of feudalism and the like, and thus, when these historical conditions altered, the situation of the serf also evolved, until his status finally disappeared. The same, however, does not apply to the dhimmi: his status was not all the product of a historical accident, but was that which *ought* to be from the religious point of view and according to the Muslim conception of the world. In other words it was the expression of the absolute, unchanging, theologically grounded, Muslim conception of the relationship between Islam and non-Islam. It is not a historical accident of retrospective interest, but a necessary condition of existence. Consequently, it is both a subject for historical research (involving an examination of the historical sources and a study of their application in the past) and a contemporary subject, most topical in relation to the present-day expansion of Islam. Bat Ye'or's book ought to be read as a book of current interest. One must know as exactly as possible what the Muslims did with these unconverted conquered peoples, because that is what they will do in the future (and are doing right now). It is possible that my opinion on this question will not entirely convince the reader.

After all, ideas and concepts are known to change. The Christian concept of God or of Jesus Christ is no longer the same for the Christians today as it was in the Middle Ages, and one can multiply examples. But, precisely what seems to me interesting and striking about Islam, one of its peculiarities, is the fixity of its concepts. It is clear enough that things change to a far greater extent when they are not set in a fixed ideological mold. The Roman imperial regime was far more susceptible to change than the Stalinist regime, because there was no ideological framework to give it a continuity, a rigidity. Wherever the social organization is based on a system, it tends to reproduce itself far more exactly. Islam, even more than

Christianity, is a religion which claims to give a definite form to the social order, to human relations, and claims to embrace each moment in the life of every person. Thus, it tends toward an inflexibility that most other forms of society have not had. Moreover, it is known that the whole of Islamic doctrine (including its religious thought) took on a juridical form. All the authoritative texts were subjected to a juridical type of interpretation, and every application (even on spiritual matters) had a juridical imprint. One should not forget that this legalism has a very definite orientation: to fix—to fix relationships, halt time, fix meanings (to give a word one single and indisputable significance), to fix interpretations. Everything of a juridical nature evolves only very slowly and is not subject to any changes. Of course, there can be an evolution (in practical matters, in jurisprudence, etc.), but when there is a *text* which is regarded in some way as an "authoritative" source, one has only to go back to that text, and the recent innovations will collapse. And this is exactly what has happened in Islam. Legalism has everywhere produced a rigidity (not an absolute rigidity, which is impossible, but a maximal one) that makes historical investigation essential. One should be aware that when one is dealing with some Islamic term or institution of the past, as long as the basic text—in this case the Koran—remains unchanged, one can always return to the original principles and ideas, whatever apparent transformations or developments have taken place, especially because Islam has achieved something that has always been very unusual: an integration of the religious, the political, the moral, the social, the juridical, and the intellectual, thus constituting a rigorous whole of which each element forms an integral part.

However, the dhimmi himself is a controversial subject. This word actually means "protégé" or "protected person." This is one of the arguments of the modern defenders of Islam: the dhimmi has never been persecuted or maltreated (except accidentally); on the contrary, he was a protected person. What better example could illustrate Islam's liberalism? Here are people who do not accept Islam and, instead of being expelled, they are protected. I have a great deal of literature attempting to prove that no society or religion has been so tolerant as Islam or protected its minorities so well. Naturally this argument has been used to condemn medieval Christianity (which I have no intention of defending), on the ground that Islam never knew an Inquisition or "witch hunts." Even if this dubious argument is accepted, let us confine ourselves to an examination of the meaning of the term *protected person*. One must ask "protected against whom"? When this "stranger" lives in Islamic countries, the answer can only be: against the Muslims themselves. The point that must be clearly understood is that the very term *protégé* implies a latent hostility. A similar institution existed in early Rome, where the *cliens*, the stranger, was always the enemy. He had to be treated as enemy even if there was no situation of war. But if this stranger obtained the favor of the head of some great family, he became his protégé (*cliens*) and was then able to reside in Rome: he was "protected" by his "patron" from the acts of aggression that any Roman citizen would commit against him. This also meant that in reality the protected person had *no genuine rights*. The reader of this book will see that the dhimmi's condition was defined by a treaty (*dhimma*) between him (or his group) and a Muslim group. This treaty had a juridical aspect, but was what we would call an unequal contract: the *dhimma* was a "concessionary charter" (cf. C. Chehata on Muslim law), something that implies two consequences. The first is that the person who concedes the charter can equally well rescind it. It is not in fact a contract representing a "consensus" arrived at by the two sides. On the contrary it is quite arbitrary. The person who grants the treaty is the only one who decides what he is prepared to concede (hence the great variety of conditions). The second is that the resulting situation is the opposite of the one envisaged in the theory of the "rights of man" whereby, by the mere fact of being a human being, *one is endowed*, automatically, with certain rights and *those* who fail to respect them are at fault. In the case of a "concessionary charter" on the contrary, one enjoys rights only to the extent that they are recognized in the charter and only for as long as it remains valid. As a person, by the mere fact of one's "existence," one has no claim to any rights. And this, indeed, is the dhimmi's condition. As I have explained above, this condition is unvarying throughout the course of history; it is not the result of social choice, but a rooted concept.

For the conquering Islam of today, those who do not claim to be Muslims do not have any human rights recognized as such. In an Islamic society, the non-Muslims would return to their former dhimmi status, which is why the idea of solving the Middle East conflicts by the creation of a federation including Israel within a group of Muslim peoples or states, or in a "Judeo-Islamic" state, is a fantasy and an illusion. From the Muslim point of view, such a thing would be unthinkable. Thus the term *protected* can have two completely opposite meanings according to whether one takes it in its moral sense or in its juridical sense, and that is entirely characteristic of the controversies now taking place concerning the character of Islam. Unfortunately, this term has to be taken in its juridical sense. I am well aware that it will be objected that the dhimmi had his rights. Yes, indeed: but they were *conceded* rights. That is precisely the point. In the Versailles Treaty of 1918, for example, Germany was granted a number of "rights" by the victors, and that was called a *Diktat*. This shows how hard it is to evaluate a problem of this kind, for one's conclusions will vary according to whether one is favorably or unfavorably predisposed toward Islam, and a truly scholarly, "objective" study becomes extremely difficult (though personally, I do not believe in objectivity in the humanities; at best, the scholar can be honest and take his own prejudices into account). And yet, precisely because, as has been said, passion is involved, studies of this kind are nevertheless indispensable in all questions concerning Islam.

So now it must be asked: is this book a serious, scholarly study? I reviewed *Le Dhimmi*, when it first appeared, in a major French newspaper[2] (the French edition was far less complete and rich than this one, especially with regard to the documents, notes, and appendices, which are essential). In response to that review I received a very strong letter from a colleague, a well-known

2. *Le Monde*, 18 November 1980.

orientalist,[3] informing me that the book was purely polemical and could not be regarded seriously. His criticisms, however, betrayed the fact that he had not read the book, and the interesting thing about his arguments (based on what I had written) was that they demonstrated, on the contrary, the serious nature of this work. First of all, he began with an appeal to authority, referring me to certain works whose scholarship he regarded as unquestionable (those of Professors S. D. Goitein, B. Lewis, and N. Stillman), that in his opinion adopt a positive attitude toward Islam and its tolerance toward non-Muslims.

I conveyed his opinion to Bat Ye'or, who assured me that she was personally acquainted with the three authors and had read their publications dealing with the subject. Given the scope of the author's researches, I would have been very surprised if this was not the case. She maintained that an attentive reading of their writings would not justify such a restrictive interpretation.

One may now ask: what were the principal arguments that our critic advanced against Bat Ye'or's analysis? He claimed, first, that one cannot generalize about the dhimmi's condition, which varied considerably. But this is precisely the point that Bat Ye'or makes in her very skillfully constructed book: using common data, from an identical basis, the author has provided documents that permit us to gain an exact idea of these differences, in accordance with whether the dhimmi lived in the Maghreb, Persia, Arabia, and so on. And although we perceive a very great diversity in the reality of the dhimmi's existence, this in no way changed the identical and profound reality of his condition. The second argument put forward by our critic was that "persecutions" to which the dhimmi was subjected had been significantly exaggerated. He spoke of "a few outbursts of popular anger," but, on the one hand, that is not something the book is particularly concerned with, and, on the other hand, it was here, precisely that our critic's bias clearly revealed itself. The "few" outbursts, in fact, were historically very numerous, and massacres of dhimmi were frequent. Nowadays we ought not to overlook the considerable evidence (which was

---

3. Professor Claude Cahen.

formerly *over*stressed) of the slaughter of Jews or Christians in all the countries occupied by the Arabs and Turks, which recurred often, without the intervention of the forces of order. The dhimmi did, perhaps, have recognized rights, but when popular hatred was aroused, sometimes for incomprehensible reasons, he found himself defenseless and without protection. This was the equivalent of pogroms. On this point, it was my correspondent who is not "scholarly." Third, he claimed that the dhimmis had personal and communal "rights," but, not being a jurist, he failed to see the difference between personal rights and conceded rights. This aspect as been stressed above and the argument is unfounded, as Bat Yeor demonstrates by a careful and convincing examination of the rights in question.

Another point raised was that the Jews attained their highest level of culture in Muslim countries, and that they regarded the states in which they resided as *their own*. With regard to the first point, I would say that there was an enormous diversity. It is quite true that in certain Muslim countries at some periods, Jews—and Christians—did attain a high level of culture and affluence, but Bat Yeor does not deny that. And, in any case, that was not anything extraordinary: in Rome, for instance, in the first century AD, the slaves (who remained *slaves*) enjoyed a very remarkable position, being active in nearly all the intellectual professions (as teachers, doctors, engineers, etc.), directed enterprises, and could even be slave-owners themselves. Nonetheless, they were slaves! The situation of the dhimmis was something comparable to this. They had an important economic role (as is clearly shown in this book) and could be "happy," but they were nevertheless inferiors whose very variable status rendered them narrowly dependent and bereft of "rights." As for the assertion that they considered as their own the states which ruled them, that was never true of the Christians. And, with regard to the Jews, they had been dispersed throughout the world for so long that they had no alternative. Yet we know that a real current of "assimilationism" came into existence only in the modem Western democracies. Finally. Bat Yeor's critic states that "a degradation of the condition of the Jews has taken place in recent times in Islamic countries," but that the dhimmis' condition ought not to be evaluated by what happened to them in the nineteenth and twentieth centuries. I can only ask whether the author of these criticisms, like so many other historians, has not given way to the temptation to glamorize the past. It is enough to notice the remarkable concordance between the historical sources referring to events, and the basic, authoritative texts to realize that such an evolution was not so considerable.

If I have dealt with the criticisms at some length, it is because I feel that is important in order to establish the "scholarly" nature of this book. For my part, I consider this study to be very honest, hardly polemical at all, and as objective as possible (always bearing in mind the fact that I belong to the school of historians for whom pure objectivity, in the absolute sense, cannot exist). *The Dhimmi* contains a rich selection of source material, makes a correct use of documents, and displays a concern to place each situation in its proper historical context. Consequently, it satisfies a certain number of scholarly requirements for a work of this kind. And for that reason I regard it as exemplary and very significant. But also, within the "living context" of contemporary history, which I described earlier, this book carries a clear warning. The Muslim world has not evolved in its manner of considering the non-Muslim, which is a reminder of the fate in store for those who may one day be submerged within it. It is a source of enlightenment for our time.

Bordeaux, May 1983.

3

Foreword to *The Decline of Eastern Christianity under Islam*[1]

Contrary to the oft-held peaceable or romanticized picture, history is not an inoffensive discipline (not to say a "science," which would be challenged immediately). Any sound historical work, that is to say, which as far as possible, avoids prejudices and preconceptions—using the maximum available sources, without selectivity other than on a scale of values according to their finality—hence, any work undertaken with conscientiousness and rigor always causes uneasiness. Actually, such a study generally challenges preconceived images of this past, as well as the traditions and judgments concerning this or that period, opinions, and, at times, ideologies, thereby giving rise to disquiet, polemics, and disputes. This has been the case with all great historical works, and the present book will be no exception.

I venture to say that it is a great historical work on account of its scrupulous examination of the sources, the search for those sources[2] (though it is impossible to speak of exhaustiveness!), and

1. Text written by Jacques Ellul in July 1991 as the foreword to Bat Ye'or, *The Decline of Eastern Christianity*. Every effort has been made to retain the essence and style of Jacques Ellul's French text.—*Miriam Kochan and David Littman, translators.*

2. On this subject, the critical section of the conclusion should be read

75

the boldness in tackling a historical factor of prime importance too often neglected. In the general current of favorable predispositions to Islam, about which I have already spoken in the preface to the author's previous book,[3] there has been a reluctance to allude to the jihad. In Western eyes, it would be a sort of dark stain on the greatness and purity of Islam. Yet this book, a sequel to the previous one, broadens considerably the perspective since it adds to the previous study of *dhimmitude* its alternative: the *jihad*. Jihad and dhimmitude are posited as an "uncircumventable" alternative: two complementary institutions, and when faced with Islam, a choice between the two has to be made! This jihad still needs to be defined: there are many interpretations. At times, the main emphasis is placed on the *spiritual* nature of this "struggle." Indeed, it would merely indicate a "figure of speech" to illustrate the struggle that the believer has to wage against his own evil inclinations and his tendency to disbelief, and so on. Each man is engaged in a struggle within himself (which we Christians know well and thus find ourselves again on common ground!); and I am well aware that this interpretation was in fact maintained in some Islamic schools of thought. But, even if this interpretation is correct, it in no way covers the whole scope of jihad. At other times, one prefers to veil the facts and put them in parentheses. In a major encyclopedia, one reads phrases such as: "Islam expanded in the eighth or ninth centuries . . ."; "This or that country passed into Muslim hands . . .". But care is taken not to say *how* Islam expanded, *how* countries "passed into [Muslim] hands . . .". Indeed, it would seem as if events happened by themselves, through a miraculous or amicable

---

most carefully: criticism of the apriorisms of a large number of historical works, criticism of the explanations given for the legitimacy of *jihad* or of the unconditional adoption of Muslim theses. But also the originality consists in noting that the majority of studies are based on what the Arabs themselves have written, without taking into account the sources originating with the subjugated and vanquished peoples. As if the former were necessarily honest and the second biased! After having so often given a hearing to Islam, why not *also* hear all those conquered, then liberated peoples of Greece, Rumania, Bulgaria, Serbia, and elsewhere? This is the great merit and one of the innovations of this book.

3. Bat Ye'or, *The Dhimmi*, (foreword by Ellul), 25–33.

operation. Regarding this expansion, little is said about jihad. And yet it all happened through war!

This book neatly highlights what one is concealing—I would say, *carefully* concealing—so widespread is the agreement on this silence that it can only be the result of a tacit agreement based on implicit presuppositions. In the face of such an agreement, this book will appear blasphemous, and will be described as polemical, simply because it reveals facts, *series* of facts, consistencies in practice—I would say a permanence, which shows that there is no question of accidental events. But despite this clarification, this book is not polemical, for the author willingly recognizes all the great achievements of the Islamic civilization, and in no way negates the values of this civilization. The author emphasizes that Islam's victories were due to the military quality of its army and the high statesmanship of its leaders. Likewise—and this is another virtue that we found in *The Dhimmi*—the author takes the greatest account of diversities and subtleties and does not globalize or generalize from a few facts. Relying on the sources to the utmost, she notes the diversities between periods and situations.

But a major, twofold fact transforms the jihad into something quite different from traditional wars, waged for ambition and self-interest, with limited objectives, where the "normal" situation is peace between peoples; war, in itself, constitutes a dramatic event which must end in a return to peace. This twofold factor is first the religious nature, then the fact that war has become an institution (and no longer an "event"). *Jihad* is generally translated as "holy war" (this term is not satisfactory): this suggests both that this war is provoked by strong religious feeling, and then that its first object is not so much to conquer land as to Islamize the populations. This war is a religious duty. It will probably be said that every religion in its expanding phase carries the risks of war, that history records hundreds of religious wars and it is now a commonplace to make this connection.[4] Hence, religious passion is sometimes expressed in this manner. But it is, in fact, "passion"—it concerns mainly a

4. See, for example, the collective book, Pierre Viaud, ed., *Les Religions et la Guerre*.

fact which it would be easy to demonstrate does not correspond to the fundamental message of the religion. This disjuncture is obvious for Christianity. In Islam, however, jihad is a religious obligation. It forms part of the duties that the believer must fulfill; it is Islam's *normal* path to expansion. And this is found repeatedly dozens of times in the Koran. Therefore, the believer is not denying the religious message. Quite the reverse, jihad is the way he best obeys it. And the facts which are recorded meticulously and analyzed clearly show that the jihad is not a "spiritual war" but a real military war of conquest. It expresses the agreement between the "fundamental book" and the believers' practical strivings. But Bat Ye'or shows that things are not so simple. Since the jihad is not solely an external war, it can break out within the Muslim world itself—and wars among Muslims have been numerous but always with the same features.

Hence, the second important specific characteristic is that the *jihad* is an *institution* and not an event, that is to say it is part of the normal functioning of the Muslim world. This is so on two counts. First, this war *creates* the institutions which are its consequence. Of course, all wars bring institutional changes merely by the fact that there are victors and vanquished, but here we are faced with a very different situation. The conquered populations change status (they became dhimmis), and the sharia tends to be put into effect integrally, overthrowing the former law of the country. The conquered territories do not simply change "owners." Rather they are brought into a binding collective (religious) ideology—with the exception of the dhimmi condition—and are controlled by a highly perfected administrative machinery.[5]

Lastly, in this perspective the jihad is an institution in the sense that it participates extensively in the economic life of the Islamic world—like dhimmitude does, which involves a specific conception of this economic life, as the author clearly shows. But it

---

5. Concerning the administrative machinery, as this book shows, it can seem somewhat disorganized, but in reality that arises from the extreme complexity of this empire (and once again this book is very "nuanced") since, in reality, there is a large degree of fundamental unity in this system.

is most important to grasp that the jihad is an institution itself; that is to say, an organic piece of Muslim society. As a religious duty, it fits into the religious organization, like pilgrimages, and so on. However, this is not the essential factor, which derives from the division of the world in the (religious) thought of Islam. The world, as Bat Ye'or brilliantly shows, is divided into two regions: the *dhar al-Islam* and the *dhar al-harb*; in other words, the "domain of Islam" and "the domain of war." The world is no longer divided into nations, peoples, and tribes. Rather, they are all located en bloc in the world of war, where war is the only possible relation with the outside world. The earth belongs to Allah and all its inhabitants must acknowledge this reality; to achieve this goal there is but one method: war. War then is clearly an institution, not just an incidental or fortuitous institution but a constituent part of the thought, organization, and structures of this world. Peace with this world of war is impossible. Of course, it is sometimes necessary to call a halt; there are circumstances where it is better not to make war. The Koran makes provision for this. But this changes nothing: war remains an institution, which means that it must resume as soon as circumstances permit.

I have greatly stressed the characteristics of this war, because there is so much talk nowadays of the tolerance and fundamental pacifism of Islam that it is necessary to recall its nature, which is fundamentally warlike! Moreover, the author provides an enlightening explanation of "Islamization," a complex process whereby Islamized populations supplanted peoples, civilizations, and religions in the conquered countries. This comprised two phases: amalgamative processes (absorption of local cultures, conversions) and conflictive processes (massacres, slavery, and so on). The conflictive and amalgamative situations could in fact coexist. Nevertheless, there are actually two phases: the first is war; the second is the imposition of the dhimmi status.

These are the foundations on which were developed both the expansion of Islam and then the evolution that resulted from the relationship of this empire with the West—an evolution that nothing could prevent and that seemed to reverse the current, since, on the one hand, the West would conquer several Islamic countries, and, on the other, Western "values" would influence this world of Islam. But if some of these values (tolerance, for example) are a sort of challenge intending to prove that Islam practices them, others act in another manner to strengthen the dominant trend: nationalism, for example. But whatever the evolution, it must never be forgotten that it can only be superficial because doctrine and conduct are based on a religious foundation: even if this may seem to be weakened or modified, nevertheless what I have elsewhere called the "persistence of religiousness" remains unchanged. In other words, even if the rites, structures, and customs are all that continue to exist of a once-strong religion—today seemingly neglected—these visible survivals only need a spark for everything immediately to revive, sometimes violently. And this process is described in a masterly fashion in this book. The situation that was thought to be dislocated and lapsed suddenly revives, and we are again faced with the fundamental choice: the world is still divided between the world of Islam and the world of war. And inside the *umma*, the only possible existence for the infidel is dhimmitude.

This leads the author to pose the question that has become so alarming today: "*Dhimmitude* of the West?" After having thus covered thirteen centuries of history, read in the light of this question, we then reach our present situation, acutely feeling its ambiguity and instability. We misunderstand this situation for lack of a clear vision of the alternative which, whether explicit or not, existed throughout these centuries, and which the present book has the immense merit to analyze rigorously. The author has the courage to examine (summarily, because this is not the purpose of the book) whether a certain number of events, structures, and situations that we know in the West do not already derive from a sort of "dhimmitude" of the West vis-à-vis an Islamic world that has resumed its war and its expansion. Hostage-taking, terrorism, the destruction of Lebanese Christianity, the weakening of the Eastern Churches (not to mention the wish to destroy Israel), and, conversely, Europe's defensive reaction (antiterrorist infrastructure, the psychological impact of intellectual "terrorism," political and legal restraints regarding terrorist blackmail): all this recalls precisely the resurgence of the traditional policy of Islam. Indeed, many Muslim governments try to combat the Islamist trend, but to succeed would require a total recasting of mentalities, a desacralization of jihad, a self-critical awareness of Islamic imperialism, an acceptance of the secular nature of political power, and the rejection of certain Koranic dogmas. Of course, after all the changes that we have seen taking place in the Soviet Union it is not unthinkable, but what a global change that would imply: a change in a whole historical trend and the reform of a remarkably structured religion! This book thus allows us to take our bearings, so as to understand more easily our present situation, as every genuine historical study should do—without, of course, making artificial comparisons, and by remembering that history does not repeat itself.

Bordeaux, July 1991.

Foreword by Alain Besançon
to *Islam et judéo-christianisme*

In 622 AD, officially in Medina, a new religion was born, which was directly opposed to the three fundamental Christian dogmas: the Trinity, the Incarnation, and the Redemption. Today, Muslims are set to outnumber Christians of all denominations put together. Over the past fifty years, three facts have dramatically changed the situation.

Muslim countries that had been dominated by the European empires (viewed as Christian by Muslims), namely the English, Russian, French, and Dutch empires, gained their independence (except for West Bank Palestine). Christian minorities still numerous at the beginning of the twentieth century, in Turkey, Egypt, and the Middle East itself, were converted, expelled (e.g., the Greeks of Asia Minor), and sometimes massacred (e.g., the Armenians). Finally, large Muslim minorities have settled peacefully in Western Europe. In France, they probably make up 10 percent of the population and according to demographers may constitute 20 percent in 20 years' time. In Germany, England, and the United States, the numbers are lower, but still significant.

This trend raises some concern in these countries. The problem is posed in relation to demography, the community, assimilation or the fight against "racism," but much more rarely in terms of religion. Indeed, for the past half-century the mood of the churches has been to promote peace and ecumenism. Although many churches seem to be in crisis—or precisely because of this crisis—we do not notice any specifically religious alarm among them. The issue for them is to welcome Islam, to seek contact, common ground, and dialogue.

In France, the establishment of the Koranic religion has been achieved quietly and incrementally. It was only recently that the French suddenly realized that it poses a very serious problem, since in the end it means the birth of another world, another civilization, within their country. In their surprise, they reacted in an uncoordinated way, as we saw during recent discussions on the acceptance or prohibition of the Muslim veil in state schools. They have the excuse that they were inadequately or badly informed. They were afraid of being charged with religious intolerance and even racism, although it is not a matter of race but of religion. Christians faced with this situation would have read literature, often written by clerics very anxious to defend the merits of Islam and to highlight the common ground that they claimed to find between this religion and their own. Such books could be seen as involuntary propaganda in favor of Islam.

This has not always been the case. Several great classical authors have demonstrated a theological incompatibility between Islam and Christianity, for instance John of Damascus and Thomas Aquinas.

Jean Mansour, known as John of Damascus, descended from a family of Byzantine officials who had played a role in the surrender of Damascus. He was initially in the service of the Caliph, in the tax department. At the first persecutions, he entered the Saint Sabbas convent, where he died in 754 AD. He wrote only a few pages, which are valuable because he is a primary witness.

His first text is included in his catalogue, *The Book of Heresies*, where Islam is classified as heresy number 100. It shows that at this time (particularly among Monophysites[1] and Nestorians,[2] who hated the Melkite[3] orthodoxy because it represented Byzantine oppression), it was not clear whether Islam was another religion or only another version of broader Christianity. This is to some extent the same today. Nevertheless, the description by John of Damascus

---

1. Monophysitism, which means "belief in one nature," is a heresy that developed in the fifth century as a reaction against Nestorianism, which also developed in the same century. Monophysitism is a doctrine that states that in the person of Jesus there was but a single divine nature. This doctrine was condemned at the Council of Chalcedon (451 AD). For rejecting Chalcedon, the Eastern church was excommunicated by the pope until 519 AD. In Syria, Egypt, and Armenia, Monophysitism dominated, and a permanent schism set in by 600 AD, resulting in the creation of the Jacobite, Coptic, and Armenian churches. National prejudices of Syrians and Egyptians against the Byzantines were a major factor in the adherence to, and extension of, Monophysitism in the early Byzantine period. The Byzantine emperors tried to eradicate Monophysitism from their empire in an effort to achieve civil and religious unity, but Empress Theodora, wife of Justinian I, promoted its spread throughout all of Syria, Mesopotamia, and other countries by sending Jacob Baradai into Syria to consecrate Monophysite bishops and to secure the foundation of the Jacobite Syrian Church. (Source: http://berchmans.tripod.com/heresy. html—*Translator*.)

2. Nestorianism is a heresy advanced by Nestorius (d. 451 AD), patriarch of Constantinople. It declared that Jesus was two distinct persons, one human, and one divine. Nestorius opposed the title of Mother of God for the Virgin Mary, contending that she was mother of the human person of Jesus. The Councils of Ephesus (431 AD) and Chalcedon (451 AD) clarified the orthodox Catholic view that Jesus' two natures are inseparably joined in one person and partake of the one divine substance. (Source: http://berchmans.tripod.com/ heresy.html—*Translator*.)

3. The Council of Chalcedon repudiated the idea that Jesus had only one nature, and stated that Christ has two natures in one person. The term *Melkite* was originally used as a pejorative term after the acrimonious division that occurred in Eastern Christianity after the Council of Chalcedon (451 AD). It was used by non-Chalcedonians to refer to those who backed the council and the Byzantine Emperor and were dubbed Melkites or *king's men* from the Aramaic word *melek*, meaning king. However, after 1724 AD, the Melkite Church was divided between the Orthodox, who continued to be appointed by the authority of the Patriarch of Constantinople until the nineteenth century, and the Catholics. It is now only the Byzantine-rite Catholics—almost exclusively Arabic-speaking and of Middle Eastern origin—who continue to use the title Melkite. (Source: http://en.wikipedia.org/wiki/Melkite—*Translator*.)

is completely sarcastic: Mohammed is a false prophet; his doctrines are absurd and can only be so because they deny Christian truths.

His later, second text appears as the *Controversy between a Muslim and a Christian*. It is a brief religious instruction to prevent Christians from converting, which they were already doing en masse. He tries to defend free will against the fatalism that he attributes to Islam, and the consistency of creation and the natural order against the capriciousness of God as understood in Islam. John speaks condescendingly, rather as a distinguished theologian of the nineteenth century would have treated the revelation of Joseph Smith and the Book of Mormon.

In this tradition of outright rebuttal, Thomas Aquinas is an important milestone. In the *Summa contra Gentiles*[4] (1:5), he sets out the following arguments: Mohammed seduced people by giving commandments that give free rein to the lust of carnal men. He imparted only truths that are easy to grasp by ordinary minds and mixed them with fables and doctrines that diminish what natural truth there is in his teaching. The validation of his doctrines rests on the power of weapons, which is not inconsistent with that of robbers and tyrants. Neither the Old nor New Testaments testify in Mohammed's favor; on the contrary, he has distorted them by legendary stories, and he forbids his disciples to read them. In short, Aquinas concludes, "those who have faith in his word, believe without due consideration."

Note that these two authors, while presenting a clear rebuttal of Islam, have both produced comprehensive explanations of Christianity. Indeed, it seems clear that any discussion with Islam requires an in-depth understanding of Christian theology and that the best way to warn faithful Christians is to educate them in their own religion, which they generally do not know well. Any controversy with Islam which is unaccompanied by religious instruction is ineffective. And instruction is what Jacques Ellul gives us in this text. It is significant that such a famous theologian speaks to us today about Islam from the most worthwhile point of view—the theological one.

4. [*Treatise against Unbelievers.*]

Jacques Ellul is a Protestant theologian. His credo is also Protestant. He follows in the tradition of Karl Barth, which has so influenced Protestant theology and, to some extent, Catholic theology in the twentieth century. When invited as an observer to the Vatican Council II, Karl Barth raised a solemn protest against a statement by the Council, which in his view did not maintain, sufficiently or clearly, that Christ was sole mediator and Savior. Thus, you will read at the same time as his critique of Islam, Jacques Ellul's confession of faith, which is the flip side, the essential counterpart, to this critique.

Unfortunately, Jacques Ellul did not have time to finish his book. The text comes from a rough draft deciphered after his death. It is very rewarding. However, I would like to tell the same story in a slightly different way, although on the majority of the points regarding Islam, I feel very close to his positions.

What status can Christian theology assign to Islam? Could it be considered a revealed religion, or a natural religion?

In good theology, Christians divide humankind like this: There is a primary division found in the covenant given to Noah. Through this covenant, they can grasp knowledge of natural law,[5] i.e., of common morality, and they can form an idea of the divine within the framework of religions we shall call pagan.

Secondarily, within this common humanity, God "chose" a man, Abraham and his "house," with whom he established a covenant. This covenant was adopted and developed in what Moses received on behalf of the people whom God "created" for himself at the foot of Mount Sinai. Finally, God in his incarnated Word came as Israel's "Messiah," and established a "New Covenant" capable of extension from Israel and its Messiah to all humanity. Within this classification, where can one place Islam?

Difficulties experienced by Christians and Jews in placing Islam in the group of natural religions come from Islam's professing belief in one God—eternal, creator, almighty, and merciful. Do they not acknowledge the first of the ten words addressed to

5. For Ellul's different viewpoint on natural law see *To Will and to Do*, chapter 3: "Morality Is of the Fall," particularly 48–49—*Translator*.

Moses, the first commandment? Yes, but this misses the point that the God of the Exodus comes as the liberator of his people in a particular historical situation: "I am the Lord your God who brought you out of the land of Egypt, the house of servitude." There is nothing of history in the creator God of the Koran. Do they then acknowledge the first item of the Christian creed, "I believe in a one God, the Almighty, creator of Heaven and Earth"? Yes, but that misses the point that this God is called Father, i.e., one who is in a personal and reciprocal relationship with humanity.

One should be aware that Muslims offer another classification: they oppose pagans to those who have "received a revelation," i.e., Jews, Christians, and Muslims. The latter are thus linked by a similarity of form (receiving a revelation) and not by a similar history.

I can now spell out my theological thesis: Islam is the natural religion of the revealed God. We classically distinguish natural religion from revealed religion. Natural religion (that of the pagans) may possibly or to some extent reach the true (i.e., revealed) God. Thus, the church, which condemns idols, nevertheless recognizes that the god that philosophy speaks of is a groping towards the true God. On the other hand, the church believes that this same God wanted to reveal himself and communicate his will for the salvation of humans, and therefore make them know truths that are beyond the resources of the human spirit. For Jews, this revelation is contained in the Bible; Christians have added a "New Testament" while acknowledging the full authority of the biblical document as it was before the coming of the Messiah.

Muslims also maintain that they have received a revelation. It is conceived of as the transmission of a pre-existing text. In this transmission, the Prophet plays no active role. He does nothing but receive texts, coming from the "Mother of the Book," which he recites as if by dictation. Unlike the Bible, which Christians claim is "inspired," the Koran is said to be the *uncreated* word of God.

Islam distinguishes between the Prophet (*nabi*), and the Messenger (*rassoul*), who is a prophet who has received a legislative message. Thus Adam, Lot, Noah, Moses, David, and Jesus were

Messengers. They were sent to specific people, but only Mohammed, "the seal of the prophets," received a universal mission.

The great Messengers from God—Moses, David, and Jesus, as literally as did Mohammed—transmitted books that were dictated to them: the Torah, the Psalms, and the gospel (in the singular). Adam, Seth, and Abraham also produced books. But, very importantly, these real or imaginary books are not held to be truthful, because their text was distorted. Jews and Christians are said to have manipulated their writings and distorted their meaning. Moreover, because the Koran contains all the truth, even if the writings of Christians and Jews were authentic, they could bring nothing new to it. This means Muslims do not recognize the value of revealed documents prior to theirs. The true Torah and the genuine gospel should not be looked for anywhere but in the Koran. The true followers of Jesus are Muslims.

So the ball is in the court of Jews and Christians. Can they themselves recognize the Bible in the Koran? The answer is no.

Is the Koran derived from the Bible? No, Muslims insist, Mohammed was illiterate. God declared to the Prophet, "You did not know the content of the Scriptures or faith before." If there are some coincidences, this is only natural, since the same message has been addressed to all "Messengers" and if there are differences, it is because Jews and Christians have truncated and distorted it.

This, Christians do not accept. Mohammed did have some knowledge of the Bible. Medina was full of Jews and Christians of various sects. John of Damascus believed there was influence from an Arian monk, others, from a Nestorian monk. For a connoisseur of the Bible, biblical figures mentioned in the Koran seem both identifiable and distorted. Abraham is not the Ibrahim of the Koran, nor is Moses, Moussa, nor Jesus, Issa. For example, Issa appears outside of space and time, without reference to the country of Israel. His mother, Mary, who is the sister of Aaron, brings him into the world under a palm tree. Then Issa performs several miracles that seem to be drawn from apocryphal Gospels. He announces the future coming of Mohammed. On the day of resurrection, he will be a witness to this.

Christians are sometimes impressed by the role Jesus plays in the Koran. But this is not the Jesus in whom they place their faith. The Jesus of the Koran repeats what earlier prophets—Adam, Abraham, Lot, etc.—had announced. Indeed, all prophets have the same knowledge and proclaim the same message, which is Islam. All are Muslim. Jesus has been sent to preach the oneness of God. He protests that he is not one who "associates" God with others: "Do not say three." He is not the son of God, but simply a created being. He is not a mediator, because Islam does not have any such concept of mediation. Since it is inconceivable for Islam that a Messenger of God should be defeated, Jesus did not die on the cross. A look-alike was substituted for him. From the Christian point of view, this Christology shows signs of a blend of Nestorianism and Docetism.[6]

To Islam the idea of a progressive revelation is foreign. The divine message was imparted to the first man, to Adam, the first Prophet. Quite simply, people forget the message and it is necessary to repeat it. Mohammed was the last Messenger and definitive reformer. The law of triumph of the Messengers and annihilation of those opposed to them is the only perspective from which history can be viewed. Islam (i.e., "submission") is the regulator which brings time back to its eternal moment, as God periodically brings humans back to his eternal decree.

Thus, to a Jew and a Christian, there is no continuity between the Bible and the Koran. Both find that the story told in the Bible appears in the Koran as fragmentary, distorted, and presented in a coherent, dogmatic matrix in such a way that the same facts appear in a different light and mean something different.

This disjunction appears just at the point where the apparent coincidence between Islam and biblical religion occurs, that of the one God, creator, almighty, and merciful. Indeed, although the Muslim likes to cite the ninety-nine names of God, these names are

6. Docetism is the belief that Jesus' physical body was an illusion, as was his crucifixion; that is, Jesus only seemed to have a physical body and to physically die, but in reality he was incorporeal, a pure spirit, and hence could not physically die. (Source: http://en.wikipedia.org/wiki/Docetism—*Translator*.)

not revealed in the framework of a covenant, as happened with the burning bush or in the gospel with the gift of the name of Father. This one God, who calls for submission, is a distant God. For Muslims, to call him Father is a sacrilegious anthropomorphism. God has condescended to send down a sacred law. He demands obedience. He does not engage in a loving relationship. The Muslim God is absolutely impassive and for him to give love would be suspect. Instead, he exhibits gratuitous condescension and kindness.

That is why Jews and Christians feel compelled to deny the Koran the status of a revelation. They also contest Islam's claim to be an Abrahamic religion.

The Abraham that Islam claims as its own is a Messenger and a Muslim. He is not the common father of Israel or of Christians who share his faith. "Abraham was not Jewish or Christian." He participated in Muslim worship in constructing the Kaaba and establishing the pilgrimage to Mecca. Rather than Mohammed having the faith of Abraham, Abraham is said to have the faith of Mohammed. Since the whole truth, according to the Koran, was given on the first day to the first man, it is inconceivable that Abraham has the founding role assigned by Jews and Christians. Muslims, in claiming Ibrahim, do not have the faith of Abraham that the history of religions seeks to reconstruct, or the faith of Abraham in the sense professed by Judaism and Christianity.

Let us now consider the opposite problem: looking at Islam as a natural religion. A common feature of natural religions is that evidence of God or the divine is everywhere. Islam, which we represent as a religion of faith, does not need faith to believe or rather to discern the evidence of God. The object of faith is not God, but God's oneness. Just as for the Greeks and Romans, so in Islam it is enough to contemplate the cosmos and the creation to be certain beyond all argument that God or the divine exists, in such a way that not to believe in him is a sign of madness, separating the unbeliever from human nature. That is not the view of Christian theology, in that reason can accept the existence of God only through investigation and reasoning. Theological faith that is supernatural comes afterwards to confirm this certainty.

For Islam, God gave a law to humans by a unilateral treaty. This law has nothing in common with the Sinaic law, which makes Israel the partner of God, nor with the law of the Spirit of which Saint Paul speaks. The law of Islam is a law external to humans, which excludes any notion of imitation of God as is found in the Bible. All that is required is to remain within the limits of the treaty, the terms of which have been laid down by God in his uncreated word and in the Sunnah or authentic tradition. Any desire to go beyond these limits is suspect. It suffices to do good and avoid evil to take advantage of the promised rewards and escape the foreseen punishments.

In this perspective, it is natural to find some pagan ethical standards. Asceticism is foreign to the spirit of Islam. Islamic civilization is a civilization of the good life. Varied sensual pleasures are permitted. There is a Muslim carpe diem, a Muslim happiness that has often fascinated Christians, just as they have felt nostalgia for the ancient world. Predestination as understood in Islam is not far from the ancient sense of *fatum*.[7] Muslims naturally relate these blessings to the perfection of their law: it is moderate, better adapted to human nature than that of the Christians, more gentle than that of the Jews. This moderation, called "religious facilitation," is seen as being to Islam's credit and makes unbelief all the more unforgivable. There is no original sin, no eternal hell for the believer.

We sometimes make fun of the Muslim notion of Paradise. This is a mistake. Admittedly, it is not like the Paradise of the Jews and Christians—a vision of God and a participation in divine life. In the Islamic heaven, God remains distant and inaccessible. However, along with peace and forgiveness humans find "satisfaction." The Bible traverses a route for humanity that begins in a garden, Eden, and ends in a city, the heavenly Jerusalem. In the Koran, humankind returns to the garden. Ancient mythologies offer us the same images of idyllic banquets where, in the same atmosphere of contentment and fulfillment of all desires, the wine runs free and the Adonises and young virgins circulate.

7. Destiny or fate.

In keeping with natural religion and the Hellenistic substratum over which Islam spread, religious life comprises different forms at different levels. For religious souls, two paths, also existing in the Greco-Roman world, open up: philosophy (the *Falsafa*[8] is permeated with Neoplatonism) and mysticism. In return for respect for the law and a token practice of the "five pillars" of Islam, less demanding souls are allowed to lead a religious life which is perfectly superficial and yet perfectly lawful and adequate. This is seen as a great advantage over the two biblical religions that in theory require more scruples and more inwardness. The stability of this superficial, legal religion is not unlike ancient religion, made up of rites that accompanied the natural and spontaneous sense of the divine.

Two facts that have always surprised Christians are the difficulty of converting Muslims and the strength of their faith, even among the most superficially religious people.

It is absurd for Muslims to become Christian, firstly because Christianity is a religion of the past, of which the best has been taken up and surpassed by Islam. But more fundamentally, Christianity seems unnatural to Muslims. They consider its ethical requirements to exceed human capacity. The Christian dogma of the Trinity worries them. It seems to exhibit *shirk,* the unforgiveable sin that gives God "associates." Christianity is suspected of being a religion of mysteries, which Islam condemns, and as such to be irrational. In contrast to this, Islam considers itself rational, as the only rational religion. This sounds threatening, because if reason characterizes human nature, the irrationalism of Christianity eliminates our human status. In this case, the *dhimmi*[9] status protects subjected Christians poorly. Muslim states, according to strict adherence to law, cannot authorize the reciprocal tolerance

---

8. *Falsafa* is a Greek loanword meaning "philosophy." (Source: http://en.wikipedia.org/wiki/Islamic_philosophy#Falsafa—*Translator.*)

9. Dhimmi are "People of the Book," protected under Islamic rule, whose status was roughly equivalent to that of medieval serfs or of Jews in Medieval Europe (see also part II, chapter 2)—*Translator.*

Appendix

asked of them by Christian states. In calling for this, Christians show their ignorance of Islam.

The strength of the Muslim faith has led to Muslims' amazement when faced with the phenomenon of modern atheism that is closely linked to the history of Christianity. As modern Christians, we tend to look at atheism as an alternative to faith. However, that was not the case in the ancient world, where Christians were accused of atheism because they refused to accept the existence of the gods. Muslim indignation is of the same nature.

Yet Christians in their encounters with Muslims have not recognized nature as they encountered it in Greco-Roman, Germanic, Slavic, and Indo-American paganism. It could be said that nature and revelation have mutilated each other. I shall not comment on the externals—the style of Muslim civic life, family structures, the status of women, and the moral code—but on something more internal which is the essence of this religion. I want to address three features.

The first is a negation of nature in its order and consistency. There are no natural laws. Atoms, accidents, and bodies only last a moment and are created by God at every moment. There is no causal relationship between two events; there are no "habits" of God. The day usually coincides with the presence of the sun, but God can change his habits and shine sunlight in the middle of the night. The miracle is therefore not a suspension of natural law, but a change in God's habits. Without the principle of causation, anything conceivable can happen. There are no causes; instead, there is a sequence, a consecutiveness. The creation of Adam does not make a case for a lineage. Like Adam, each person is created "anew." "He created you in your mother's womb, creation after creation."[10] Each moment of growth is the subject of a new creative act. In the eyes of the West, the Muslim view of the cosmos seems to be deficient in its stability, with a God whose nature and purpose are concealed, with time broken up into a series of moments unconnected with one other, and with nature suspended by the

10. Koran, Sura 39:6—*Translator.*

94

"habits" of the Almighty. There is no longer any boundary between reality and dream.

The second feature we have seen is the denial of history. The Bible is a history. Revelation proceeds by steps. God intervenes in history by words and acts whose memory is preserved by tradition and by an inspired book, which is constantly subjected to interpretation. The Koran is uncreated, and there is no interpretative magisterium. It does not contain a history, but stories. God intervenes by protecting the prophets who are infallible and perfect, and by destroying their enemies. Since the same message is invariably conveyed by all the Messengers, the sense of history is that of an endless repetition of the same lesson. There is no innate difference between the present, the past, and the future.

A third feature touches on religious virtue. Moral virtue is found in natural religions as in revealed religions and according to Cicero, it "offers its ceremonies and its care to a higher nature that we call divine." In all religions, religious virtue governs piety, prayer, worship, sacrifices, and other similar acts. Even if one rejects the authenticity of the Koranic revelation, it seems difficult not to relate the Muslim faith to a specific form of religious virtue. What promotes confusion is that under Islam this virtue may be pushed beyond what is acceptable in biblical religion. In biblical faiths, people are in fact responsible for their affairs within a physical, social, and political framework, which has its own consistency and its appropriate laws. Religious duties are therefore limited to a reasonable area, within or beyond which believers sin by default or by excess. The idea of natural order has not the same strength in Islam where God's interest extends to secondary as well as to primary causes. Religious virtue can therefore be so intense and broad that Jews or Christians would consider it beyond the happy medium.

To conclude: we understand better our initial problem, which was the misunderstanding that faces Christians when they approach Islam. Christians are struck by the religious impetus of the Muslim towards a God that they recognize willy-nilly as being their God. But they do not recognize themselves—not in this distant God, nor in the relationship that the Muslim has with him. Christians are used to distinguishing worship of false gods, which they call idolatry, and worship of the true God, which they call true religion. To deal with Islam adequately we would need to forge a difficult concept, which could be described as *idol worship of the God of Israel*.

Let us return to the contemporary historical situation. Islam is growing and seems no more attracted by Christianity today than in the past. On the contrary, Christians are subjected to its attraction and may even be tempted by it.

This attraction is obvious in a scholar, Louis Massignon, who influenced in no small way the Christian vision of Islam in the twentieth century. He established in some theological circles two vigorous opinions: Firstly, that the Koran is in its own way a revelation, without doubt cut down and primitive, but still a revelation of what is substantially the biblical essence. Secondly, it then follows, that Islam is genuinely, as it claims for itself, of Abrahamic lineage.

When we consider that in our bookshops the literature favorable to Islam is generally written by Christian priests of Massignonian lineage, we can see that the attraction to Islam derives from several feelings. A certain critique of our liberal, capitalist, individualist, competitive modernity finds beauty in traditional Muslim civilization, to which it attributes contrary facets: stability of traditions, community spirit, and warmth of human relations. Church people, thrown into a panic by the cooling of the faith and practice in Christian countries, particularly in Europe, admire Muslim devotion. They marvel at these people who, in the desert or in an industrial shed in France or Germany, prostrate themselves five times a day for ritual prayer. They think that it is better to believe in something rather than in nothing at all, and they imagine that since they believe, they believe in almost the same thing. They confuse faith and religion. Finally, they are happy to note the important role Jesus and Mary play in the Koran, without being aware that this Jesus and this Mary are homonyms that have only the names in common with the Jesus and Mary they know.

This last point is serious because it interferes with the relationship between Christians and Jews. In this Christian perspective, Muslims seem "better" than Jews do, since they honor Jesus and Mary, whom Jews do not. Thus, Judaism and Islam have parallels drawn between them, with Islam appearing to have an advantage. Jews also draw a parallel between Christianity and Islam, with Islam, having a less problematic monotheism, again appearing to have an advantage. However, Christians cannot seriously accept this comparison, and the Catholic Church has expressly condemned it. If it were accepted, it would mean renouncing their lineage from Abraham, the prophetic role of Israel, and the Davidic lineage of the Messiah; it would transform Christianity into a message independent of time and cut off from its source, from its history. The gospel then would become another Koran and would dissolve in its universalism. This is why it is necessary to expurgate from contemporary Christian discourse dangerous phrases such as "three Abrahamic religions," "three revealed religions," and even "three monotheistic religions" (because there are many others). The most false of these expressions is "three religions of the Book." It does not mean that Islam is referring to the Bible, but only that Islam has provided a legal category—"the people of the book"—for Christians, Jews, Sabeans, and Zoroastrians. To these they can apply the status of *dhimmi*, i.e., subject to discrimination, protecting their lives and their property instead of killing and enslaving them as promised to *kafir* and pagans.

That one so easily uses such expressions is a sign that the Christian world is no longer capable of clearly distinguishing between its religion and Islam. Are we back to the time of Saint John of Damascus, when they wondered if Islam was not another form of Christianity? It is not out of the question. For the historian, it is a well-known situation. When a church no longer knows what it believes, or why it believes it, it slides imperceptibly towards Islam. Overwhelmingly and in a short time, this happened to the Monophysites of Egypt, the Syrian Nestorians, the Donatists of North Africa, and the Arians of Spain.

Christians have made a great mistake in considering Islam as a simplistic, elementary religion, a "religion of cameleers." On the contrary it is an extremely strong religion, a specific *crystallization* of the relationship of man to God, completely different to that of the Jewish or Christian faith, but no less coherent. Christians are also wrong to suppose that Islam's worship of the one God of Israel makes Muslims closer to them than the pagans. In fact, as evidenced by the history of their relations, they are more radically separated due to the mode of worship of the same God. Two religions separated by the same God. It follows that if Christians want to understand Muslims and enter into "dialogue" with them, as we say today, they must rely on what remains of natural religion, of the natural virtue within Islam. And above all, they must rely on the common human nature they share with them. But the Koran, unlike Homer, Plato, or Virgil, cannot be regarded as a *praeparatio evangelica.*[11]

Jacques Ellul does not address the problem exactly as I have just explained it. We know and he repeats it here, that following Karl Barth, he denies Christianity the status of a "religion." I want to highlight this point of theology, although it is not necessary to explore it here, as it does not alter at all the way we look at Islam. I would be happy if Jacques Ellul could resume the discussion today! However, this text is the last he wrote. He felt that before leaving this world in 1994, he urgently needed to give it quite a solemn warning. It must be read as a testament. Today, ten years on, we understand its gravity better.

Alain Besançon

11. "Preparation for the Gospel"—*Translator.*

Bibliography[1]

Citations in This Edition

Barth, Karl. *Church Dogmatics*. Edited by G. W. Bromiley and T. F. Torrance; translated by A. T. Mackay and T. H. L. Parker. Edinburgh: T & T Clark, 1936–1977.

Bousquet, G. *L'Éthique sexuelle de l'Islam*. Paris: Maisonneuve, 1966. [*Sexual Ethics in Islam*.]

Chastenet, Patrick. *Sur Jacques Ellul, un penseur de notre temps*, Colloque international sur le thème «*Technique et société dans l'œuvre d'Ellul*,» 12 et 13 novembre 1993, Institut d'études politiques de Bordeaux, Editions L'Esprit du temps, 1994. [*On Jacques Ellul, a Thinker of our Time*. Proceedings of the International Symposium on *"Technology and Society in the Work of Jacques Ellul,"* 12—13 November 1993.]

Chouraqui, Andre. *Les dix commandements aujourd'hui: dix paroles pour réconcilier l'Homme avec l'humain*. Paris: Pocket, 2005. [*The Ten Commandments today: ten words to reconcile Man with the human being*.]

Eliade, Mircea. *Histoire des croyances et des idées religieuses. Volume 3, De Mahomet à l'âge des Réformes*. Paris: Payot, 1983. [*History of Religious Beliefs and Ideas*. Volume 3, *From Mohammed to the Reformation*.]

Ellul, Jacques. *An Unjust God? A Christian Theology of Israel in Light of Romans 9—11*. Translated by Anne-Marie Andreasson-Hogg. Eugene, OR: Wipf & Stock, 2012.

———. *Histoire de la propaganda*. Paris: PUF, 1967; reprinted 1976. [*History of Propaganda*.]

———. *Israël: Chance de civilization*. Paris: Éditions Première Partie, 2008. 4. [*Israel: Civilization's Lucky Break*.]

1. Some minor bibliographical notes in the French original have been omitted or simplified in line with the Wipf & Stock standard. The equivalent English titles of untranslated French publications is given in [square brackets] after each publication.—*Translator*.

Bibliography

————. *Propaganda: The Formation of Men's Attitudes*. Translated by Konrad Kellen and Jean Lerner. New York, NY: Knopf, 1965.

————. *Reason for Being: A Meditation on Ecclesiastes*, Translated by Joyce Main Hanks. Grand Rapids, MI: Eerdmans, 1990.

————. *The Ethics of Freedom*. Translated by Geoffrey W. Bromiley. Grand Rapids, MI: Eerdmans, 1976.

————. *The Subversion of Christianity*. Translated by Geoffrey W. Bromiley. Grand Rapids, MI: Eerdmans, 1986.

————. *To Will and to Do: An Ethical Research for Christians*. Translated by C. Edward Hopkin. Boston, MA: Pilgrim Press, 1969.

————. *Un chrétien pour Israël*, Monaco: Editions du Rocher, 1986. [*A Christian for Israel.*]

Ellul, Jacques, ed. "Islam et Christianisme," *Foi et Vie* (a special issue), 1983. ["Islam and Christianity"—a special issue of *Faith and Life.*]

Lavignotte, Stéphane. *Jacques Ellul: L'espérance d'abord.* Lyon: Editions Olivétan, 2012. [*Jacques Ellul: Hope First.*]

Pirenne, Henri. *Mahomet et Charlemagne.* Paris: Payot, 1937. [*Mohammed and Charlemagne.*]

Sourdel, Dominique. *L'Islam médiéval.* Paris: PUF, 1979. [*Medieval Islam.*]

Sourdel, Dominique, et Janine Sourdel. *Dictionnaire historique de l'Islam,* Paris: PUF, 1996. [*Historical Dictionary of Islam.*]

Viaud, Pierre, ed. *Les Religions et la Guerre Judaïsme, Christianisme, Islam.* Paris: Cerf, 1991. [*Religions and War: Judaism, Christianity, Islam.*]

Volf, Miroslav. *Allah: A Christian Response.* New York: HarperOne, 2012.

Ye'or, Bat. *The Decline of Eastern Christianity under Islam. From Jihad to Dhimmitude: Seventh to Twentieth Century.* Foreword by Jacques Ellul. Translated by Miriam Kochan and David Littman. Rutherford, NJ: Fairleigh Dickinson University Press /Associated University Press, 1996.

————. *The Dhimmi: Jews and Christians under Islam.* Translated by David Maisel, Paul Fenton, and David Littman. Foreword by Jacques Ellul, 25–33 Rutherford, NJ: Fairleigh Dickinson University Press /Associated University Press, 1985.

Bibliography

Other Books and Articles by or about Jacques Ellul

Chastenet, Patrick. *Jacques Ellul on Politics, Technology, and Christianity: Conversations with Patrick Troude-Chastenet.* Translated by Joan Mendès France. Republished Eugene, OR: Wipf & Stock, 2005.

———. *Lire Ellul: Introduction a l'œuvre socio-politique de Jacques Ellul.* Presses universitaires de Bordeaux. [*Reading Ellul: Introduction to the Socio-Political Work of Jacques Ellul.*]

Ellul, Jacques. *A Critique of the New Commonplaces.* Translated by Helen Weaver. New York, NY: Knopf, 1968.

———. *Anarchy and Christianity.* Translated by Geoffrey W. Bromiley. Grand Rapids, MI: Eerdmans, 1991.

———. *Autopsy of Revolution.* Translated by Patricia Wolf. New York, NY: Knopf, 1971.

———. *Betrayal of the West.* Translated by Matthew J. O'Connell. New York, NY, The Seabury Press, 1978.

———. *Changer de révolution. L'inéluctable prolétariat,* Paris: Le Seuil, 1982. [*Revolutionary Change and the Unchangeable Proletarian Condition.*]

———. *Conférence sur l'Apocalypse de Jean,* Nantes: Éditions de l'AREFPPI, 1985. [*Conference on the Apocalypse of John.*]

———. *De la révolution aux révoltes,* Paris: Calmann-Lévy, 1972 [*From Revolution to Revolt.*]

———. *Déviances et déviants dans notre société intolérante,* Toulouse: Eres, 1992. [*Deviance and Deviants in Our Intolerant Society.*]

———. *Essai sur le recrutement de l'armée française aux XVIe et XVIIe siècles.* Mémoire de l'Académie des sciences morales, (prix d'Histoire de l'Académie française), 1941. [*Essay on the Recruitment of the French Army in the 16th and 17th Centuries.* Memoir of the Academy of Moral Sciences, (prize in history from the Académie Française).]

———. *Étude sur l'évolution et la nature juridique du Mancipium* (law doctorate thesis), Bordeaux: Delmas, 1936. [*Study on the Evolution and the Legal Nature of Mancipium.*]

———. *False Presence of the Kingdom.* Translated by C. Edward Hopkin. New York, NY, The Seabury Press, 1972.

———. *Histoire des institutions,* Paris: PUF: t. I et II: L'Antiquité, 1951; t. III: Le Moyen Age, 1953; t. IV: XVIe—XVIIIe siècles, 1956; t. V: XIXe siècle, 1957. Republished in the "Droit fondamental" collection, PUF, 1991. [*History of Institutions:* Vols I and II: The Ancient World, 1951; Vol. III: The Middle Ages, 1953; Vol. IV: The Sixteenth to Eighteenth Centuries, 1956; Vol V: The Nineteenth Century, 1957.]

———. *Hope in a Time of Abandonment.* Translated by C. Edward Hopkin. New York, NY, The Seabury Press, 1973.

———. *In Season and Out of Season: An Introduction to the Thought of Jacques Ellul.* (Based on interviews by Madeleine Garrigou-Lagrange). Translated by Lani K. Niles. San Francisco, CA: Harper & Row, 1982.

Bibliography

————. *Introduction à l'histoire de la discipline des Eglises réformées de France*, published by the author, 1943. [*Introduction to the History of the Discipline of the Reformed Churches of France.*]

————. *Jesus and Marx: From Gospel to Ideology*. Translated by Joyce Main Hanks. Grand Rapids, MI: Eerdmans, 1988.

————. *Jeunesse délinquante: Une expérience en province* (in collaboration with Yves Charrier), Paris: Mercure de France, 1971. [*Juvenile Delinquents: A Provincial Experiment.*]

————. *La Genèse aujourd'hui*, Nantes: Éditions de l'AREFPPI, 1987. [*Genesis Today.*]

————. *La Pensée marxiste, Cours professé à l'Institut d'études politiques de Bordeaux de 1947 à 1979*, Paris: published in the "Contretemps" collection, La Table Ronde, 2003. [*Marxist Thought: A Course Given at the Bordeaux Institute of Political Studies from 1947 to 1979.*]

————. *L'Empire du non-sens: l'art et la société technicienne*, Paris: PUF, 1980. [*Empire of Non-Sense: Art and the Technological Society.*]

————. *Les Combats de la liberté*, Geneva: Labor & Fides, Paris: Le Centurion, 1984. [*The Fight for Freedom.*]

————. *L'Homme à lui-même*, correspondence. Jacques Ellul et Didier Nordon, Paris: Éditions du Félin, 1992. [*Reflections on Humanity:* Correspondence of Jacques Ellul and Didier Nordon.]

————. *Living Faith: Belief and Doubt in a Perilous World*. Translated by Peter Heinegg. San Francisco, CA: Harper & Row, 1980.

————. *Métamorphose du bourgeois*, Paris: Calmann-Lévy, 1967; republished in the "La Petite Vermillon" collection, La Table Ronde, 1998. [*Transformation of the Middle Class.*]

————. *Money and Power*. Translated by LaVonne Neff. Downers Grove, IL: InterVarsity, 1984.

————. *Oratorio: les quatre cavaliers de l'Apocalypse?* Pessac: Opales, 1997. [*Oratorio: The Four Horseman of the Apocalypse?* (An epic poem.)]

————. *Prayer and Modern Man*. Translated by C. Edward Hopkin. New York, NY, The Seabury Press, 1979.

————. *Presence of the Kingdom*. Translated by Olive Wyon. New York, NY, The Seabury Press, 1967.

————. *Silences: Poèmes*, Pessac: Opales, 1995. [*Silences: Poems.*]

————. *Si tu es le Fils de Dieu. Souffrances et tentations de Jésus*, Zurich: EBV, Paris: Bayard-Le Centurion, 1991. [*If You are the Son of God: The Suffering and Temptations of Jesus.*]

————. *The Apocalypse: The Book of Revelation*. Translated by George Schreiner. New York, NY, The Seabury Press, 1977.

————. *The Humiliation of the Word*. Translated by Joyce Main Hanks. Grand Rapids, MI: Eerdmans, 1985.

————. *The Judgement of Jonah*. Translated by Geoffrey W. Bromiley. Grand Rapids, MI: Eerdmans, 1971.

Bibliography

————. *The Meaning of the City,* Translated by Dennis Pardee. Grand Rapids, MI: Eerdmans, 1970. Republished Wipf & Stock, 2011.

————. *The New Demons.* Translated by C. Edward Hopkin. New York, NY, The Seabury Press, 1975.

————. *The Political Illusion.* Translated by Konrad Kellen. New York, NY: Knopf, 1967.

————. *The Politics of God and the Politics of Man.* Translated by Geoffrey W. Bromiley. Grand Rapids, MI: Eerdmans, 1972.

————. *The Technological Bluff.* Translated by Geoffrey W. Bromiley. Grand Rapids, MI: Eerdmans, 1990.

————. *The Technological Society.* Translated by John Wilkinson. New York, NY: Knopf, 1964.

————. *The Technological System.* Translated by Joachim Neugroschel. New York, NY: Continuum, 1980.

————. *The Theological Foundation of Law,* Translated by Marguerite Wieser. New York, NY, The Seabury Press, 1969.

————. *Violence: Reflections from a Christian Perspective.* Translated by Cecelia Gaul Kings. New York, NY, The Seabury Press, 1969.

————. *What I Believe.* Translated by Geoffrey W. Bromiley. Grand Rapids, MI: Eerdmans, 1989.

Porquet, Jean-Luc. *Jacques Ellul: L'Homme qui avait presque tout prévu.* Paris: Le Cherche-Midi, 2003. [*Jacques Ellul: The Man Who Foresaw Almost Everything.*]